Killing

Lazarus

Discover Why The Enemy Is Trying
To Take You Out And What You Can
Do About It

Ryan Bruss

DEDICATION

This book is dedicated to all God's children who have put up with the devil for long enough. I wrote this book to share with you the revelation of why the enemy has been trying to take you out and what you can do about it! You are loved, cherished and adored by Father God. He believes in you and the plans that He has purposed in His heart for you before the world was formed. Beloved, I am believing that everything is about to change in your life.

"And we know that all things work together for good to those who love God, to those who are the called according to His purpose." Romans 8:28

ACKNOWLEDGMENTS

Approximately one year before this book was published, I was sitting in a meeting in Georgia where Dr. Kevin Zadai was ministering. He was sharing about Lazarus, and how the religious leaders wanted to kill him because many believed in Jesus on account of him. It was then that this book was downloaded to my spirit. Thank you, Kevin and Kathi, for being such a major part of my life! Thank you to my wife Megan, for supporting me as I locked myself away to write this book and for looking over the final manuscript. Thank you to Crystal Harden for all the effort you put into proof reading and editing. Thank you to all those who call Antioch Community Church your home—love you all!

And of course, thank you Jesus for Your love for me and allowing me to carry Your beautiful heart to the world.

KILLING LAZARUS

CONTENTS

ENDORSEMENTS

This book is alive! In fact, as I read *Killing Lazarus*, written by my son-in-law Ryan Bruss, it felt as if the words were pulsating on my screen. I could feel the Spirit moving on him as he wrote, and I could see the impact this book would have on the readers. If every born-again believer in America would read this book, the whole Church of America would also be pulsating with life. Read this book, learn to sit at Jesus' feet, and you will never be the same.

> --Dr. Michael L. Brown, host of the Line of Fire radio broadcast, president of FIRE School of Ministry

Killing Lazarus is a book for this hour. I loved it! Every page is filled with encouragement, hope and conviction. Pastor Ryan does a masterful job exposing the devil's agenda for your life, as well as, the Father's heart for each of us. Believe me, you will find yourself totally engaged with the eternal truths found in this book. Well done Pastor Ryan!

> --Todd Smith, Christ Fellowship Church, North Georgia Revival

Supernaturally empowering! This book is fiercely exposing and destroying the work of the serpent who's hiding in our blindsides to hinder our calling and destiny. It is empowering us to be bold in our identity, go deeper in our intimacy with God to become an unstoppable conqueror. Your life is never going to be the same after reading it. It is so needed in such a time as this to take you to the next level as you were praying for so long. You're going be empowered and activated beyond your expectations.

> --Isik Abla - Pastor, Author and TV & Social Media Evangelist

Wouldn't it be amazing to have a book that revealed all of the sneaky tactics of the enemy? Have you ever experienced your battle intensifying right before the breakthrough? Well, I have great news for you, because Ryan Bruss, in his brand new book, Killing Lazarus, will empower you to stand strong and strengthen you for the battle. Ryan unwraps the truth of who you are before God and why there is a battle for your destiny. He will give you equipping tools straight from the Word of God and these truths will help you in every single season. This is a book we should all have in our hearts and in our own personal libraries.

--Julie Meyer, Song Writer,
Author of Singing The Scriptures, Dreams & Supernatural
Encounters, Founder of Into The River
Intotheriver.net

Through the pages of this book you will find the Spirit of wisdom and revelation on how to become an overcomer through Jesus Christ! The keys of understanding and knowledge that Pastor Ryan offers will make you more than a conqueror in the character and power of the Lord Jesus! Prepare yourself for heavenly insights that will cause you to rule over the enemy by the presence and power of the Holy Spirit!

--Tony Kemp,
Tony Kemp Ministries

Ryan Bruss is a magnificent author, teacher, pastor, and above all, friend. Ryan is known to bring such great revelation from the heavens to the earth in such a simple manner for every believer to understand. His book, *Carrying The Presence* was a tremendous tool to the Body of Christ. I know this book, *Killing Lazarus*, will bless your spirit as well.

--Prophet Tracy Cooke

The Lord has such an incredible destiny for you! Do you truly believe that though? Life can beat us all up sometimes, and the enemy can bring on confusion and discouragement. Jesus is our anchor for a life of hope and true lasting joy. This book *Killing Lazarus* will nudge you to come forth out of old ways of thinking and being and come up higher into the greatness that God has for your life. His genuine caring heart to really help people step into their destiny, seeps through this excellent book by Ryan Bruss.

--Ana Werner, Founder of Ana Werner Ministries
President, Eagles Network
Author of The Seer's Path, Seeing Behind the Veil,
The Warrior's Dance, co-author, Accessing the Greater Glory
www.anawerner.org

Knowing how to fight back against the enemy of our soul is urgent. In the last days it will become our most vital skill. The last thing God wants for us is to be powerless when there is so much power available, or to be without authority when so much was won for us on the cross of Christ. How do we fight back and defeat the enemy? That question is crucial. Jesus yearns to give you power, authority, and skill, not only to match the enemy, but to destroy his works. God means for us to thrive not survive. This book is for this season of warfare. It is for every child of God. He lays a recipe for victory. And, he does it clearly, simply and convincingly. Ryan Bruss' book Killing Lazarus will flood you with hope, answers, and power to stand against anything.

--Mario Murillo, www.mariomurillo.org

Foreword

I remember my heavenly visitation with the Lord Jesus Christ in 1992. After showing me how the spirit realm operates so clearly, I realized that I did not want to leave Jesus and the heavenly realm to go back to the earth. Jesus had opened my eyes to see what was really going on behind the scenes and it was clear that satan was at war with the saints continuously. I was shown how we could win against these evil spirits and the specific battle strategies of the enemy. However, I also saw the intensity of the situation and what it would take for a believer to win and go into what I call "overthrow".

Jesus showed me what He had accomplished for all believers in order to win against the plans of the enemy. He had brought forth such a great salvation for us. However, I saw that most believers did not engage the Lord on the level in which Jesus had obtained for them in order for us to be victorious. I saw the intensity that we would have to have in order to stay in victory and not be deceived. The intensity was a lot greater than what the established church had portrayed, unfortunately.

I remember being told by Jesus that He was saddened because believers were not asking to walk in holiness in this life so that they could walk on the sapphire floor in the throne room with Him, but were wanting to stay on the fence called "lukewarm" between the world and heaven, just barely making it to their heavenly home after they passed from this life.

Because of the revelation of what I was shown concerning the demonic, I did not want to come back because I saw that the believer was not being taught correctly and they did not discern that it is the believers responsibility to engage with intense warfare against these demons continually. I observed that the level of excellence that was required to combat these entities was not achieved in this generation. I knew that even if I did come back to the earth, that it would be difficult for me to get believers on the same page in order to understand what is involved and living out this life victoriously.

I have been told by religious leaders that there is not a demon behind every tree. I thought about this as I was standing with Jesus with my eyes wide open to the warfare and I thought, "those religious leaders were right, there is not a demon behind every tree there are five." Actually, it is easier to take out the tree to get to the five demons hiding behind it! This sounds funny but it is actually profoundly serious as well as true.

So, anytime you can read a book like my friend Ryan Bruss wrote, you should learn as much as you can about the other realm. You need to acquire from those who have seen and heard from the other side. It is needed in this day in order to shift a whole generation's mindset so that we finish correctly and timely on our mission here on this earth. Enjoy!

Kevin L. Zadai

Founder and President of Warrior Notes and Warrior Notes School of Ministry

1

COME FORTH!

"Forgive me for being so ordinary while claiming to know so extraordinary a God." Jim Elliot, missionary/martyr

I believe that nothing is ever going to be the same for you again—I mean that. A trusted seer/intercessor has held this manuscript in her hands and prayed for all those that will read this book and felt hope coming back to your life! Things are about to turn for you and your family. The life that you have been living up until now may have felt disappointing and disjointed but everything is about to shift as you embrace what God wants to reveal to you. The enemy has been messing with your life long enough!

I feel like one of the biggest issues with many believers today is that they are utterly confused about life—about the Christian life that is. If God is so great and so good and so wonderful, how come my life is in such turmoil? How come I am always sick? How come my husband left me? Why is my child on drugs? Why don't I ever have any joy? How come I never seem to have enough money to get ahead? Why did my life turn out the way it did? You may have asked these very questions or ones like them. These are sincere questions from sincere Christians.

I do not have the answers to all your life questions (and some things we will never fully understand until we are with Jesus in Heaven), but here's what I do have: I have learned a few secrets—and they're the reasons *why* the devil is trying to take you out and what you can start doing about it. It's the same reason that devil wanted to *kill Lazarus* (see John 12:10-11). Once you receive this revelation, it will bring such understanding, refreshing and hope to your heart that you will live completely different than you are right now. You're going to make the enemy pay for what he's done or even tried to do to you and your loved ones.

More on that later...

For now, let's pick up the story of Lazarus where he had just died:

"Now a certain man was sick, Lazarus of Bethany, the town of Mary and her sister Martha.

When Jesus heard that, He said, '"This sickness is not unto death, but for the glory of God, that the Son of God may be glorified through it."' Now Jesus loved Martha and her sister and Lazarus. So, when He heard that he was sick, He stayed two more days in the place where He was.

So when Jesus came, He found that he had already been in the tomb four days...

Jesus said to her, '"I am the resurrection and the life. He who believes in Me, though he may die, he shall live. And whoever lives and believes in Me shall never die. Do you believe this?"'

Then Jesus, again groaning in Himself, came to the tomb. It was a cave, and a stone lay against it. Jesus said, '"Take away the stone."'

Martha, the sister of him who was dead, said to Him, '"Lord, by this time there is a stench, for he has been dead four days."'

Jesus said to her, '"Did I not say to you that if you would believe you would see the glory of God?"' Then they took away the stone from the place where the dead man was lying. And Jesus lifted up His eyes and said, '"Father, I thank You that You have heard Me. And I know that You always hear Me, but because of the people who are standing by I said this, that they may believe that You sent Me."'

Now when He had said these things, He cried with a loud voice, "Lazarus, come forth!" And he who had died came out bound hand and foot with graveclothes, and his face was wrapped with a cloth. Jesus said to them, '"Loose him, and let him go."' John 11:1, 4-6, 17, 25-26, 38-44

Now *that's* a miracle! And guess what? You are also a miracle! I'm not talking about what your life may look like or feel like right now (I'm going to get to that). I'm talking about the fact that, just like Lazarus, you were also once dead, but now you are alive! You are born again!

Let me share with you what *just* happened in between writing these paragraphs. I went to a place to eat lunch where I have been going a couple of times a week for several years, and this has never happened until today. As I was walking in the store, someone in a car literally tried to run me over! It was the craziest thing. It was as if they were aiming for me! The devil is upset at what is about to happen to you through this book.

Friends, there are reasons why the enemy is trying to take us out. The enemy doesn't like us, which is an understatement to say the least. My son and I were recently eating at a pizza place, and there was a group of people (college age) sitting at the table across from us. They were drunk and acting crazy. We ignored them as they weren't doing anything to us directly. All of a sudden, one of the girls started swearing profusely, and I felt an evil spirit that was on her turn and look at me as if to say, "How did you like that?". Our very presence was disrupting the party of those evil spirits. Demon spirits do not like Christians—especially those who are making a difference for the Kingdom of God. I talk about this at length in my book, *"Carrying the Presence"*. As a Christian, everywhere you go matters because you belong to Jesus. Always remember that.

Back to the story of Lazarus...

As you read in the story, Lazarus was dead. And not just dead—he was *really* dead! I mean, four days in the tomb dead.

What were the circumstances in your life before you became a Christian? Were you hooked on drugs? Were you promiscuous? Were you a thief? Were you a cold-hearted businessman? Maybe you were living for the next moment to find another high? Did you grow up in church? Perhaps you didn't get into too much trouble before you were born again. Or maybe you were saved at a young age like me. Whatever the case may be, let me tell you something: Before you met Jesus, you were dead. I'm not talking about physically dead, but dead from the inside out. Friends, without Jesus, we are lost.

However, the good news is:

"...you He made alive, who were dead in trespasses and sins, in which you once walked according to the course of this world, according to the prince of the power of the air, the spirit who now works in the sons of disobedience, among whom also we all once conducted ourselves in the lusts of our flesh, fulfilling the desires of the flesh and of the mind, and were by nature children of wrath, just as the others.

But God, who is rich in mercy, because of His great love with which He loved us, even when we were dead in trespasses, made us alive together with Christ (by grace you have been saved), and raised us up together, and made us sit together in the heavenly places in Christ Jesus, that in the ages to come He might show the exceeding riches of His grace in His kindness toward us in Christ Jesus.

For by grace you have been saved through faith, and that not of yourselves; it is the gift of God, not of works, lest anyone should boast. For we are His workmanship, created in Christ Jesus for good works, which God prepared beforehand that we should walk in them." Ephesians 2:1-10

You and I *were* dead just like Lazarus. And then Jesus called for you. And in a sense, He told you to come forth! Don't you just love that? Can you picture Lazarus coming out of that tomb with his graveclothes still wrapped around him?

Beloved, now that you are a Christian, you are not the same as you were before you were saved.

"Therefore, if anyone is in Christ, he is a new creation; old things have passed away; behold, all things have become new." 2 Corinthians 5:17

Now, to put it bluntly, why don't we act or live like we are saved? Why aren't we living as ones who were once dead and are now alive from the inside out? What happened? What happened to the joy of our salvation? What happened in our walk with God? What happened to that person who came out of darkness? I know what happened, and that's why I wrote this book for you.

Here's a *now* word for you: Jesus is calling you again to COME FORTH!

You may feel beat up, bruised, wounded, exhausted and want to give up and that's just what the enemy wants you to do—give up. Beloved, Christians do not give up; they press on, they push through, they overcome, they win. All because the Greater One is living inside us (see 1 John 4:4).

You *are* going to make it. You *will* fulfill the call of God on your life. You will oppose the enemy and make him pay for all that he and his minions have done to your life.

I am not telling you all of this to simply give you some superficial pep talk. We have enough of that going on in our churches. There is a lot of yelling, screaming, declaring and decreeing in our pulpits today, but believers are going home without being changed from the inside out. They are not being given the tools to come against the enemy and win over and over again.

As a pastor, I've had to make the decision to not give the people of our church what they want, but what they need. Ask any pastor—that's not always easy to do, because you feel the pull to help them get through the week by preaching a good uplifting message, and there is nothing wrong with that in and of itself. However, what they *really* need, and what *you* need, is to know how to overcome, live in victory, walk in joy and love and fight like a true warrior when nobody else is around. It's time to move beyond living from one church service to the next, hoping you will survive the week. It's time to live bold, strong, free and full of love, joy and peace every day.

Listen, you got this. You are going to make it in this world as a Christian. You are going to be so on fire for God that the enemy is not going to know what to do with you. You are called of God. He has a plan for your life. The enemy does not want you to fulfill that plan and wants to take you out early. The devil wants to make you ineffective and wounded so that you don't have any more strength to fight. What he never counted on was that you were going to have the revelation on how to fight back and win against him.

If you are born again, you have Jesus living inside, and you cannot fail. It's impossible to fail, because Jesus never fails, and He is with you wherever you go. So today, I am telling you—prophesying to you—to come forth! Do you hear the voice of Jesus calling you out of your tomb like He called out Lazarus?

COME FORTH—and take off those graveclothes.

COME FORTH—and repent of any sin.

COME FORTH—and begin again.

COME FORTH—and let Me heal your body.

COME FORTH—and let Me restore you.

COME FORTH—and let Me set you free.

COME FORTH—and let Me bless you.

COME FORTH—and let Me wipe away your tears.

COME FORTH—and let Me heal your broken heart.

COME FORTH—and I will take away the shame.

COME FORTH—and follow Me.

COME FORTH—and live in My love.

"Through the LORD'S mercies we are not consumed, because His compassions fail not. They are new every morning; Great is Your faithfulness." Lamentations 3:22-23

The very first reason why the enemy is trying to take you out is because you, my friend, are born again! The devil hates the fact that you have given your life to Jesus. He hates that he lost you and that you will spend an eternity with your heavenly Father. Because of the hate that he feels for you, he will try to steal, kill and destroy you (see John 10:10), and at the very least, he will do whatever it takes to cause your life to be ineffective for the Kingdom of God.

So, don't be surprised that the enemy is trying to take you out! Because:

"...you were washed, but you were sanctified, but you were justified in the name of the Lord Jesus and by the Spirit of our God." 1 Corinthians 6:11

When was the last time that you thanked Jesus for your salvation and the great price that He paid for you to be redeemed?

"Let the redeemed of the LORD say so, whom He has redeemed from the hand of the enemy." Psalm 107:2

The enemy hates the redeemed. He hates the fact that you don't belong to his kingdom any longer. You need to understand that the very fact that you belong to God keeps the enemy after you. Why? Because you are now a threat to him. Believe me, the enemy knows how much you know and how well you know it. He knows that if he can get you to misunderstand God's heart for you or get you to backslide and walk away from God, he can pull you back into his world. However:

"...lest Satan should take advantage of us; for we are not ignorant of his devices." 2 Corinthians 2:11

We know what the enemy is up to; we are not unaware of what he's trying to do. When you said yes to Jesus and no to the devil's kingdom, you became marked for life. What do you think happened after Lazarus was raised from the dead?

"Now a great many of the Jews knew that He was there; and they came, not for Jesus' sake only, but that they might also see Lazarus, whom He had raised from the dead. But the

chief priests plotted to put Lazarus to death also, because on account of him many of the Jews went away and believed in Jesus." John 12: 9-11

Did you catch that? The chief priests wanted to kill Lazarus because many of the Jews were believing in Jesus because of him. And it's the same today. You are a walking testimony of the salvation of Jesus in your life. And just like Lazarus, many people will believe in God and follow Him because of your life. It's not about being an evangelist or even part of the five-fold ministry. It's about a changed life. It's about being a Christian. Your life has been changed from the inside out. You came out of that "tomb", and now here you are like Lazarus, sitting and fellowshipping with Jesus and that irritates the devil. I don't know about you, but I take great joy in irritating the devil. And to make it worse for him, we remind him that we are bought by the blood of Jesus and that our eternal home is in Heaven, and his eternal home is in hell.

Now that you are born again, your very existence infuriates him. However, it's very important to realize that now that you are saved, he is trying to work his way into your life to minimize any threat you would be to his kingdom. I will talk more about this later, but he will try to take you out with sickness, offense, depression, financial hardship, sin, family problems, etc. Again, he knows he lost you and that you are now born again and desire to live for Jesus, so he will try to take you out in other ways.

Sometimes we have to go back to the beginning, take a deep breath, and simply thank Jesus for our salvation and praise His name because He has saved us from the wrath of God. When was the last time you worshipped and thanked Him just because you are privileged to be His son or daughter?

The devil hates Jesus. He hates God's children. He hates Christians. You are a Christian—that's the very first reason why the enemy is after you.

You were created in the very image and likeness of God (see Genesis 1:26-27). You are Father's son. You are Father's daughter. You have an inheritance in God (see 1 Peter 1:4). Rejoice today that your name is written in the Book of Life!

"He who overcomes shall be clothed in white garments, and I will not blot out his name from the Book of Life; but I will confess his name before My Father and before His angels." Revelation 3:5

That verse alone should get you up in the morning and cause you to dance and praise your way through the day! If you are born again, your name _____ (write your name!) is written in Heaven right now!

"For the Christian, Heaven is where Jesus is. We do not need to speculate on what Heaven will be like. It is enough to know that we will be forever with Him." William Barclay

KILLING LAZARUS

2

YOUR SUPERNATURAL CALLING

"Expect great things from God; attempt great things for God." William Carey, pioneer missionary to India

You have been called by God to accomplish His purposes through your life in your generation. It doesn't matter what you have been through, what you're going through now or what you will go through in the future—God has a beautiful plan for your life. Everything is going to work out for you in this life if you learn to simply yield to His heart and His plan for your life.

The current circumstances that you are facing—no matter how dire—is not the end of your story. There is so much more that God has for you. There is a call of God on your life that you are destined to fulfill.

Because we know that:

"...all things work together for good to those who love God, to those who are the called according to His purpose"
Romans 8:28

When Paul wrote this verse by the unction of the Holy Spirit, he said that *all* things work together for good. And all means all—even the bad things that have happened in your life. All of us have had bad things happen in our lives that have caused us to question God and if He even knows or remembers that we are still here on this earth "going through it". The truth is, He does know, He does care, He loves us beyond measure, and He is with us until the end. He has not forsaken us, nor has He forgotten about us. Bad things do happen to us, yes, but He is not the author of those bad things. The author is your adversary, and he is:

"...walk[ing] about like a roaring lion, seeking whom he may devour." 1 Peter 5:8

That is not one of those "feel good verses". Rather, this verse has a "bite" to it if you are not watchful.

You see, another reason why the enemy is trying to take you out is because of the plans and purposes that God has for your life. You ARE called. Whether you feel it or believe it right now does not change the fact that while you are on this earth, God has a specific plan for your life.

After Lazarus was raised from the dead, what do you think he was talking to everyone about? What do you think his message was? I'm sure Lazarus was like, "Jesus is real, and He is really, really powerful!" His life was radically changed, and don't you think that when Jesus was sitting with him that He was teaching Lazarus what to do with this powerful testimony? As far as I know, we don't have any historical record of what happened to Lazarus later on in life, but I'm sure he told everyone, everywhere how wonderful and powerful Jesus of Nazareth was. No one was going to ever talk him out of his testimony! And you have a testimony. Whether you grew up in church or got saved yesterday on the streets of New York—you have a testimony. And your testimony will always be part of your calling.

Listen to what God said to young Jeremiah regarding his calling:

"Then the word of the LORD came to me, saying: '"Before I formed you in the womb I knew you; Before you were born I sanctified you; I ordained you a prophet to the nations."' Jeremiah 1:4-5

Don't you think that when the word of the Lord came to Jeremiah, the devil was taking notes? I'm convinced that from that moment on, the enemy was carving out his own plan for Jeremiah's life. You see, when the enemy knows to a certain degree what you are called to do, he will do everything he can to redirect you from that calling. He tries this with EVERY Christian. In the enemy's mind, there is no way that he is going to let you march through this life fulfilling God's plan. He will try to find a way to get between your salvation and God's plan. If he can't take your soul, he will try to take your destiny. He doesn't want you to affect his kingdom in any way whatsoever. But the enemy is scared. He's nervous. Why is he nervous? Because in the back of his mind, he knows that if you stand up and declare that no matter what, you are setting your heart towards the Son, and that you will do those things that God has called you to do in love, you will become unstoppable.

Beloved, please never forget that before you were ever born, God established a plan for your life, just like Jeremiah. This plan—this call on your life is greater, more rewarding and more fulfilling than you could ever imagine. You may not fully know what that plan is right now, and that's ok—you will. God knows, and He is working behind the scenes and within your heart to set you up to bring you into those things that He has called you to do. At the end of this chapter, I will give you a list of a few things that will help you begin to know what God has called you to do.

King David also knew that he was called before he was born:

"For You formed my inward parts; You covered me in my mother's womb. I will praise You, for I am fearfully and wonderfully made; Marvelous are Your works, and that my soul knows very well.

My frame was not hidden from You, when I was made in secret, and skillfully wrought in the lowest parts of the earth. Your eyes saw my substance, being yet unformed. And in

*Your book they all were written, the days fashioned for me, when as yet there were none of them. How precious also are Your thoughts to me, O God! How great is the sum of them!"
Psalm 139:13-17*

You know the story; David was anointed at a young age as a shepherd, but didn't become king until many years later. Between being anointed by the prophet Samuel as a boy and actually sitting on the throne of Israel, he had to fight a lion, a bear, a giant, the Philistines, the Amalekites, King Saul and his men, his own wife, Michal, and even his own heart. But none of these things stopped him from reigning over Israel. He knew it was the destiny on his life. He was not perfect; he sinned greatly, we know that, but through David's life, a man after God's own heart, God raised up Jesus:

"And when He had removed him [Saul], He raised up for them David as king, to whom also He gave testimony and said, "I have found David the son of Jesse, a man after My own heart, who will do all My will.' From this man's seed, according to the promise, God raised up for Israel a Savior— Jesus." Acts 13:22-23

David loved God deeply and was committed to the call on his life no matter what the circumstances looked like. I want to encourage you to read the life of David and all of the corresponding Psalms that he penned during the good times and the bad. You can literally read how the enemy was trying to redirect and disqualify David his entire life. But always remember that David loved well, and that's how he made it through. He knew His God, and that was his foundation no matter how surrounded he was by the enemy.

I am privileged to be a volunteer Chaplain with the Charlotte, North Carolina Police Department. With my busy schedule, I try to make sure that I ride-along with the police once or twice a month. One of my best friends is a police officer with the department, and he is on fire for God.

What I am about to tell you, these police officers see firsthand every single day, and I also see it every time I am on a call with them. Just the other day (when I was riding with my friend that loves the Lord), we had a call to an apartment where someone had called about a female roommate that attempted suicide by overdosing on pills. When we got to the apartment, the medics were helping this young lady get down the stairs and into the ambulance. She could barely walk and was basically incoherent because of all the harm she had done to her body. As they were helping her down the stairs, she admitted to everyone that she drank alcohol and mixed it with pills to harm herself. She also said that she was a stripper, and I believe she may have also been a college student. So here was this beautiful young lady that was a student, a stripper and suicidal. I would imagine that when she was a little girl, dreaming big dreams, she never imagined that she would be in this place in life. We didn't get a chance to minister to her as she was whisked away to the hospital, but our hearts broke for her—this was NOT the plan that God has for her life. Somewhere, whether from her upbringing or her own choices, the enemy got in, and he is trying to take her out. (Pray for her with me). There is a call of God on her life! She just hasn't found Jesus yet. She's not called to be addicted to drugs and strip in front of men. She's called to be a daughter of Father God and change a generation! It reinforced to me that we have to be responsible Christians and bring Jesus to the broken, the unsaved, the hurting, the sick and the dying.

From that call, the dispatch told us that they were receiving many calls of a woman that was acting strangely walking in the road with a hospital bag in her hand. When we pulled up to the area, the woman was spinning in circles in a parking lot as she was obviously high on something. As we approached her, I was somewhat taken aback. She had the hospital bag in her hand, was wearing only one shoe, and was dirty and full of sores, but her face was very beautiful as she spoke to us with intense eyes. Even now as I am telling you this story, my heart is heavy for her as this is not why this woman was born into this world. She was breathed into her mother's womb, all the days of her life were written about her (Psalm 139), and she belongs in the Kingdom of God. But right now, she's addicted to drugs. Thankfully, I was able to minister to her for some time. I gave her one of the business cards to my church and told her that there are ladies at our church that would love to meet her. She knew about Jesus but had no relationship with Him. Do you see how the enemy is just looking to take people out as quickly as he can? Please pray for her that she will come to our church and get help. Once again, when this precious woman was a little girl, she didn't ever dream that she would be where she is today. The enemy has been trying to take her out—she's called of God.

From that call, the dispatch led us to another location where a young man was high and causing problems at a gas station. When we got to the location, he was at the street corner, high, with no shoes on, acting crazy. We were able to talk to him for a little while, and there were obvious father issues based on what he was telling the officers. This young man was a good-looking kid, and the enemy was stealing his heart and was trying to make a mess of his life. When he was little, he never dreamed that he would be in the back of a police car one day. He is called by God, just like the two women I mentioned. (Please pray for him also).

These three people are called of God as you are also called of God. Father has a plan for everyone's life. If we are going to see the call of God fulfilled in our lives, we must keep our foundation strong in God's love, power, and promises. When we do that, we can make it through anything in this life. Stay very, very close to Jesus my friends, and you will fulfill the destiny that's on your life.

Now, if you are like many Christians that I meet, sometimes the last thing you want to be reminded of is the call of God on your life. Why? Because you feel like you are just trying to get through the day, let alone God's plan for your life. And I can certainly understand that you may feel that way. You just have to know that you feel that way because the enemy has gotten in and disrupted your life to the point where you feel like you want to give up and give in. You feel stuck. You feel sick and tired of being sick and tired. I get that. However, you are still called. There is still a plan and purpose for your life. Period. And I know that in your heart of hearts, you want to do those things that God has called you to do. It just seems hard to comprehend right now because of all that has gone on in your life.

I am privileged to be the lead minister of our church, Antioch (www.antiochcommunitychurch.org), here in North Carolina. We have a unique mission to help people get to their destination and calling in God. Here's what I say on our website:

"The Lord gave me a vision several years ago that our Antioch Community will be like a '"train station"' for '"training"'.

The Lord showed me that it would be as if Antioch was a train station and a train would drop off passengers at our door—it would be their next '"stop"' in life. People from all walks of life and diverse backgrounds would be coming through our door. Old and young, rich and poor, the outcasts of society, those hungry for more of God, entire families, college students, first responders, the broken, the wounded, the sick, the forgotten, evangelists, pastors, teachers, prophets, apostles and everyone in between.

People would get off the train with all their '"baggage"', bring it into the church and lay it at the feet of Jesus. This is when our community will love on you, pray for you, pray you through and help you get delivered, set free and set on fire for God. We will pray for miracles in every area of your life— your body, your marriage, your finances, your destiny, or whatever area you need a touch from God.

Our desire is for you to be radically changed from the inside out and in every area of your life so you can do those things that God has called you to do! We will love you, disciple you, equip you, impart to you and train you for your assignment in this life.

There will be many people that will come to Antioch and stay for years and years, but there will also be many that will come for a season, and then we will help put them '"back on the train"' to their next destination in life. However, these people will be completely different from when they first came to Antioch. They will get back on the train to go plant a church, head to the mission field, or move to a new location and live on fire for God—but each one that is willing will go into all the world and share the Good News, heal the sick, raise the dead, cast out devils and fulfill the destiny on their lives!"

Friends, each one of us will stand before God one day to give an account for not only *how* we lived our lives but *what we did* with our lives for God's glory.

"For we must all appear before the judgment seat of Christ, that each one may receive the things done in the body, according to what he has done, whether good or bad." 2 Corinthians 5:10

The enemy has been fighting and fighting with you because he doesn't want you to ever fulfill all that God has called you to do. You have to begin to understand that one of the main reasons why the enemy is trying to take you out is because you are called of God!

And of course, the call of God varies from one person to the next. I see this within my own household (I have a family of four) and my extended family. We may not always know in full what each one of us is supposed to do for God, but we:

"...press on, that I may lay hold of that for which Christ Jesus has also laid hold of me. Brethren, I do not count myself to have apprehended; but one thing I do, forgetting those things which are behind and reaching forward to those things which are ahead, I press toward the goal for the prize of the upward call of God in Christ Jesus. Therefore let us, as many as are mature, have this mind; and if in anything you think otherwise, God will reveal even this to you" Philippians 3:12-16

Friend, you have to press on. You have to push through. You have to run your race and finish your course (see 1

Corinthians 9:24-27 and 2 Timothy 4:7). I pray that you understand at this point that you have a destiny on your life, no matter what. You may be struggling in your marriage, your health, your finances and so on. However, beloved, that does not change the fact that you are still called. That destiny may seem a million miles away right now, but that's why I wrote this chapter—that's why I wrote this book. Everything is about to shift for you.

Paul certainly knew the divine paradox of being called by God and "going through it" at the same time. Here's proof:

"...I speak as a fool—I am more: in labors more abundant, in stripes above measure, in prisons more frequently, in deaths often. From the Jews five times I received forty stripes minus one. Three times I was beaten with rods; once I was stoned; three times I was shipwrecked; a night and a day I have been in the deep; in journeys often, in perils of waters, in perils of robbers, in perils of my own countrymen, in perils of the Gentiles, in perils in the city, in perils in the wilderness, in perils in the sea, in perils among false brethren; in weariness and toil, in sleeplessness often, in hunger and thirst, in fastings often, in cold and nakedness—besides the other things, what comes upon me daily: my deep concern for all the churches." 2 Corinthians 11:23-28

"I know how to be abased and I know how to abound. Everywhere and in all things I have learned both to be full and to be hungry,

both to abound and to suffer need. I can do all things through Christ who strengthens me." Philippians 4:12-13

It's Christ who strengthens you, dear one. Therefore, you will get through what you need to get through to fulfill the call of God on your life. Reading what Paul went through makes me feel like we can get through anything life tries to throw at us. And remember:

"...we are more than conquerors through Him who loved us. For I am persuaded that neither death nor life, nor angels nor principalities nor powers, nor things present nor things to come, nor height nor depth, nor any other created thing, shall be able to separate us from the love of God which is in Christ Jesus our Lord." Romans 8:37-39

If you feel like you have gone too far or avoided the call of God too long or sinned too greatly that God cannot use you, that's a lie that the enemy has imbedded in you that needs to be rooted out. It's never too late to start right now.

"For the gifts and the calling of God are irrevocable" Romans 11:29

Just know that the devil will try to come between you and your spouse. He will try to keep you sick and in pain. He will try to get you offended and bitter. He will try to keep you in financial bondage. He will lie to you and say it's too late to start right now. He will try and say anything he can to discourage you to the point that you lose sight of your destiny.

Let me give you a snapshot of my own life to illustrate this. From a young age, I would have dreams from the Lord at night that spoke to me about my calling. At around 12 years old, I knew that I knew that I had a call of God on my life to preach the Gospel. Do you know who else knew that? The enemy.

At 12 years old, I lost my father to cancer (he had battled it for five years prior to his death), and as you can imagine, that was a huge blow to our family. Being the oldest of three, I carried false responsibility for years with a wounded heart because of his early death. We also didn't have much money at all—we were poor. You can see this illustrated on an episode of *It's Supernatural!* with Sid Roth. None of this changed the fact that I was called of God to preach the Gospel.

As I became a teenager, I started hanging around with the wrong crowd like a lot of broken young people do. I did things that were wrong and sinful, while all the time, the Holy Spirit was tugging on my heart. The heaviness of my heart, depression and bitterness was so bad that suicidal thoughts tried to make an entrance in my mind. However, none of this changed the fact that I was still abundantly loved by Father God and called to preach the Gospel.

I never walked away from God, but I was not in a good place in my heart, because the enemy was sowing lies in my mind that were trying to get me to run to the world and away from God. My heart needed to be healed, forgiven, cleansed and restored.

At 18 years old, while living on my own (by the way, I have an on fire, praying mom, that like the persistent widow in Luke 18, never left Jesus alone about her kids!), the only way I can describe it is that my heart began to warm towards God again, and He was doing something very gentle and loving within me. It was during this time that I went to a small church meeting where a prophet was ministering. During the ministry time, this prophet said, "Young man, stand up. The Lord is doing a new thing in you. He's turning you inside out and upside down, but the one thing that He's not doing, is turning you loose..." The prophecy went on for quite a while, but I remember it like it was yesterday, and that was almost 30 years ago. The Lord said that I was called to the nations and that I would make an impact, that there would be no lack of provision, and on and on it went. I left that meeting and never looked back again. The Lord didn't give up on me, and that did something to my young heart. I truly was called to preach the Gospel.

Have you received a prophetic word about your calling? Many of you have. That word is still just as strong over you today as when you received it. Always remember this: when God called you (before you were even born), He factored in all the crazy things that would happen to you in life and the crazy decisions you were going to make. He knew you were going to one day run to Him with your whole heart. He knew you were going to go through some hard times. But He also knew you were going to make it.

Sadly, even though God wants everyone with Him in Heaven (see 2 Peter 3:9), some choose Hell. And many who ran from the call of God rather than embracing it will make it to Heaven, but there will be little to no reward for them there. Let's not be like that. There is a great reward in Heaven that awaits the sons and daughters of God that pay the price to obey God and love others authentically from the heart while on this earth. I saw this reward system in Heaven (you can read about this encounter in my book, *Carrying the Presence*).

Almost immediately at 19 years old, I became a youth pastor in the inner city of Minneapolis, MN and ministered on the streets on a regular basis. I had a fire burning in me for God and for souls. At the same time, my heart was also burning for the nations. At the time, my friend Brad and I shared a third-floor apartment together that was directly under the flight pattern of the airport. Dozens and dozens (if not hundreds) of times, I would stand on our deck at night and watch those airplanes fly overhead, and I would thank the Lord that He was sending me to the nations, that the money would be in my hands for me to go, and that the people would receive me when I got there. I sowed much prayer into my calling and destiny as a young man. Well, at the time of this writing, I am 46 years old, and I have been to over 20 countries (and some of those countries I have traveled to many times, like Israel where I have been privileged to have gone nine times). And the total cost that I have had to pay is $500.00! That's it! All of those countries, and I have personally only paid $500.00. Only God can do that!

When God calls you, He equips you and then makes sure the provision is there for you to fulfill that call. That doesn't mean that each trip overseas has been easy—not at all. The enemy hates it when I get on a plane to go preach the Gospel, but you still go when God says go. The enemy will try to keep you broke and in lack so you never accomplish all the wonderful things that God has for you to do. All of your needs are already met in the eternal provision of God before you ever take your first step towards your destiny. God never asks you to do something for Him and then not provide for you. That doesn't mean you don't pray and intercede, do warfare, raise money and walk by faith. That's all part of the process. The point is, where He guides, He provides.

"And my God shall supply all your need according to His riches in glory by Christ Jesus." Philippians 4:19

Jesus is with you hand in hand, leading you into your destiny. On one of my trips to Guatemala with some friends, it was my turn to preach on a particular night. We drove on a rocky road filled with potholes up a mountain, passing a few people on the way up. I thought to myself that there was really not going to be anyone at the top of this mountain to hear me preach. When we finally arrived at the top, to my surprise, there was a very large church building nestled into the mountain. I wondered where all the people were going to come from to fill the church? This place was in the middle of nowhere! We went to the back of the church and ate before the meeting and when we came out to the sanctuary, there were at least five hundred people crammed in. There were beautiful people peering in every window and standing all around the outside waiting to hear the preacher from America.

I will never forget that as the music began playing, several people came to the front of the church and started acting crazy. Women were literally picking up their babies and hurling them through the air, and they would land at the front of the altar! We had never seen anything like it before. It was because witchcraft had infiltrated the church. I sat down during worship and started to pray and wondered how this was all going to turn out. How do I preach to a bunch of demon-possessed church people? Immediately this verse spoke loud in my spirit:

"...and lo, I am with you always, even to the end of the age."
Matthew 28:20

Ok, God, You've got this. I will preach for you Jesus. You called me to do this. It was time for me to share and as I preached, it was translated into Spanish and then Quiche' (a Mayan language) and then back to me again. Looking out at all the beautiful faces, I said out loud, "Jesus, You are welcome here." Then all hell broke loose. You see, Jesus was finally welcomed in this church, so when He walked in, the demons manifested. It took our team at least 20 minutes to calm down the crowd!

I preached the Gospel and gave the altar call, but only a small number of people came forward. That didn't seem right to me. I turned to look for the pastor behind me, and he was gone. I slipped out through a side door to find him, and there he was laughing and counting all the money that came in the offering! Through a translator, I asked the pastor what he was doing. I said this is life and death out there! We talked for about five minutes, and he was so convicted by the Holy Spirit that he came out to the stage, got down on his knees and repented for allowing witches to come and affect the church. We gave another altar call together, and nearly the whole crowd of people came to the altar to repent. It was so beautiful.

The next night we held another crusade in a different city, and the same pastor from the night before brought a busload of people from his church. The faces of every single person were beaming with the glory of God. I can see their faces even now as I tell you this story.

Friend, you may not be called to preach, but you are still called. Whether you are a preacher, plumber, politician, prophet, painter, pediatrician, pastor, plasterer or piano player makes no difference. Your calling is just as important as mine. What God has called you to do on this earth is very important to the Kingdom of Heaven. You are called to bring the Kingdom of God to whatever sphere of influence you are a part of in this life. That's why the enemy is trying to stop you from fulfilling your destiny. You play an important role in God's eternal plan.

My wife and I have been married for over 21 years with two wonderful kids who are heading into what God has called them to do. During these past 21+ years, my wife and I have been through the good, the bad and the ugly, as most marriages have. But at the end of the day, my wife and I have never gotten our eyes off of what God is calling us to do. We have cried together, laughed together, gotten mad at each other, and forgiven each other. We deeply love each other and are committed to staying the course with God as we continue to head towards our destiny.

When it comes to *your* calling, here's what you can do right now. First, you must identify all the areas in your life where the enemy has tried to get you off track from what God has called you to. One by one, give those things to the Lord. If you have to repent, then repent. Start declaring that no matter what your finances are shouting at you, no matter what the doctor's report says, no matter what your circumstances are trying to tell you, you will go all the way with God. I know things may feel like a mess right now, and the devil wants you to feel overwhelmed by everything. But remember, that's one of his tactics—to try to convince you that it's impossible to move towards your destiny with all that's going on in your life. He tries to create scenarios in your life to make you feel distant from God and to make you feel that you are unloved and that the promises in God's Word don't work for you. All those are lies.

"What then shall we say to these things? If God is for us, who can be against us?" Romans 8:31

Are you breathing? Then there is hope. You still have time to yield to God and His plan for your life! Beloved, whatever is standing in the way of your calling, it's time to deal with it and put the devil on the run! Find someone you trust to help pray you through, but know this, every promise in the Word of God belongs to you. That's why I am convinced you're going to make it—because His Word says you will. Again:

"...all things work together for good to those who love God, to those who are the called according to His purpose." Romans 8:28

Father is full of love, mercy, power and joy towards you. Jesus has already won, and now He's trying to win you over to execute the victory through your life!

Ok, so how do I know what I am called to do? Below is a list of a few practical ideas that you can apply to your life that will help you become awakened in your spirit with what God is calling you to do:

SEE YOURSELF IN THE BIBLE

As you read the Bible, what verses seem to always jump off the page at you? What Scriptures really stir your heart? As wonderful as the entire Word of God is, many times certain Scriptures leap off the page at us because the Holy Spirt is confirming through the Word a direction we are supposed to go in regards to our destiny.

YOUR PASSION

What are those things that you are most passionate about in life? Maybe it's something that you have always desired to do in life such as being a police officer, owning your own business, becoming a missionary, building houses, starting an orphanage, and the list goes on. Many times, what you're passionate about is in line with what God has called you to do. For instance, you may have always had a real empathy and compassion for people, so you feel a pull in your heart to be a nurse, social worker or minister (the list is obviously too big to suggest here). The key is to realize that it's not *just* about *what* you are supposed to do in this life but it's about *how* the Lord is going to use you as an ambassador for Him in your place of influence. God puts passion within us for what He is calling us to do (again no matter what it is) and then expects us to bring His Kingdom to those particular areas.

"Now then, we are ambassadors for Christ, as though God were pleading through us: we implore you on Christ's behalf,

be reconciled to God." 2 Corinthians 5:20

I believe that many people in these last days are going to have full-time jobs, but then God is going to use them in other areas of influence to bring His Kingdom. In other words, just because you are passionate about social and moral issues (such as the fight against abortion, human trafficking, adoption, homelessness, poverty, education, etc.) doesn't mean that you are to quit your "day job" to pursue those things. Work and provide for your family and ask God how He can use you to pursue the passions of your heart at the same time. I am not called to be a police officer (I have always loved working with first responders), but the Lord opened a door for me to be a volunteer chaplain with the police so I am able to fulfill that desire in the midst of everything else I am doing. It's the same for you. Pray for open doors for you to pursue the desires of your heart for the glory of God. And always remember, Father knows best. If a door does not open for you, it may not be time for you to walk into those things quite yet. Don't get discouraged. It's about timing, your character development and the Father's will. Just don't lose your passion for those things.

GIFTS AND TALENTS

What are you gifted or talented at? Maybe you play an instrument like the piano. Did you ever think that even though you are a schoolteacher, maybe God is wanting you to produce a soaking cd for your friends to help them encounter God in the secret place (see Psalm 91)? Maybe you are talented at doing odd jobs around the house. Did you ever think that even though you sell insurance, maybe God is wanting you to minister to those who don't have much money, to help them fix some things around their house that have been weighing them down? I will tell you this: if you are gifted and talented in certain areas, God does not intend for you to keep those things to yourself, but also to be a blessing to others. Maybe you are a stay-at-home parent and are gifted in drawing, painting or crafts. Why not talk to the leadership at your church and see if there is a way you can teach art to others in the church for the glory of God?

STAY CLOSE

One of the greatest ways to begin to know what you are called to do is by staying very close to the heart of God by continually abiding in His presence. When we lean in close to Jesus, He whispers to us and tells us those things we were created to accomplish. There have been many, many times I have received direction in my calling from the Lord by simply spending time with Him and allowing His heart and passion to become my heart and passion. The Lord wants to get us to the place where we are obeying all that He is asking us to do. Sometimes there is a delay in the next step in our calling because we haven't yet obeyed the last step! If that's you, ask the Lord to forgive you, and go bàck to the last step and walk in obedience. Intimacy with God is the greatest key in receiving His passionate, fiery heart for you and for what He has called you to do.

"I am the vine, you are the branches. He who abides in Me, and I in him, bears much fruit; for without Me you can do nothing." John 15:5

WHAT'S ON FATHER'S HEART?

No matter what you are called to do, you can start right now with reaching those that are dear to the Father's heart. We shouldn't ever have to be told to do this, as it is part of our spiritual makeup as born again believers. Our spirits are alive and ignited with the people that Father God is running after. To be honest with you, the reason why many Christians struggle with reaching out to the world around them is because they are too focused on their own issues, rather than the precious life of someone else.

When we learn to yield our lives to God and abandon ourselves to Him, He ministers to the deepest places within us, heal us, sets us free, restores our hearts and sets us on fire *for the lost, hurting and broken*. So, who is on Father's heart? Please read the Scriptures below and allow the presence and power of God to touch your heart with His heart:

"Pure and undefiled religion before God and the Father is this: to visit orphans and widows in their trouble, and to keep oneself unspotted from the world." James 1:27

"For I was hungry and you gave Me food; I was thirsty and you gave Me drink; I was a stranger and you took Me in; I was naked and you clothed Me; I was sick and you visited Me; I was in prison and you came to Me.'

Then the righteous will answer Him, saying, "Lord, when did we see You hungry and feed You, or thirsty and give You drink? When did we see You a stranger and take You in, or naked and clothe You? Or when did we see You sick, or in prison, and come to You?" And the King will answer and say to them, 'Assuredly, I say to you, inasmuch as you did it to one of the least of these My brethren, you did it to Me.'" Matthew 25:35-40

"The Spirit of the LORD GOD is upon Me (and friends, the Spirit of the Lord is upon YOU right now!), because the LORD has anointed Me to preach good tidings to the poor; He has sent Me to heal the brokenhearted, to proclaim liberty to the captives, and the opening of the prison to those who are bound; To proclaim the acceptable year of the LORD, and the day of vengeance of our God; To comfort all who mourn, to console those who mourn in Zion, to give them beauty for ashes, the oil of joy for mourning, the garment of praise for the spirit of heaviness; That they may be called trees of righteousness, the planting of the LORD, that He may be glorified." Isaiah 61:1-3

"And as you go, preach, saying, 'The kingdom of heaven is at hand.' Heal the sick, cleanse the lepers, raise the dead,

cast out demons. Freely you have received, freely give."
Matthew 10:7-8

If we would just understand how good God is, how much He is for us, how the enemy has tried to take us out because of the calling and destiny on our lives and that we are *already* anointed to do what God has called us to do, we would never doubt again that we each have a divine purpose in this life.

THE MINISTRY OF LOVE

If you would simply love and serve others well—the second greatest commandment—you will have a multitude of open doors to minister to people. It's what I call, "The Ministry of Love." It doesn't matter what you are specifically called to do in this life, all of us are called to love deeply from the heart (see Romans 13:8 and 1 Peter 1:22). In Heaven, we will be rewarded with how well we loved on earth. So, no matter where you are at in your understanding of what you are called to do, I can promise you that it will begin and end with loving and serving people!

"And the second, like it, is this: 'You shall love your neighbor as yourself…'" Mark 12:31

"just as the Son of Man did not come to be served, but to serve, and to give His life a ransom for many." Matthew 20:28

SOW INTO YOUR DESTINY

What you can do right now, no matter how old you are or how long you have been a Christian, is to sow into your future—the destiny and call of God on your life. The number one way you sow into your future is by praying into it, just like I did when I was 19 years old in that apartment. Much of what I am doing today for God is because I sowed into my future through prayer 5, 10, 20, 30 years ago. When we pray into our destiny and thank the Lord that His will *will* be done through our lives, He will see to it that it happens. It's important to remember to never, ever give up on yourself as God Himself never, ever gives up on you. Again, He has already factored in everything that we will go through (the good, the bad and the ugly) in life, because He has already been to our future. It's never too late to follow after God's heart *with all of our hearts.*

We can also sow into the call of God on our lives by becoming excellent in our spirit (see Daniel 5:12). Set yourself apart right now with whatever you are doing in life by doing everything as unto the Lord (see Colossians 3:23). People around you will take notice, and more importantly, God will take notice of your diligent heart. The enemy will try to discredit you to others and cause you to feel like everyone is out to get you or that no one ever appreciates what you do, whether it's at work, church or simply going about your life. Stay the course anyway. Don't worry about what other people think about you. You're heading to a destination that was ordained by God before the foundations of the world.

"A man's gift makes room for him, and brings him before great men." Proverbs 18:16

We also sow into our future by being good students of the Word of God.

"Be diligent to present yourself approved to God, a worker who does not need to be ashamed, rightly dividing the word of truth." 2 Timothy 2:15

You don't have to be a preacher to study God's Word. Every Christian should diligently study God's Word, no matter what you are called to do. The Word of God never fails and is your blueprint for the call of God on your life. Never forget that. Your story is written within the pages of God's story. The Holy Spirit will lead you to the life of David or Esther or the disciples or in the epistles, etc., and you will continually have "aha" moments as what you are reading is what you are needing at any given moment. Again, the Word of God is your guide to the call of God on your life. It is very important to always keep this in mind.

Another very important way to sow into your future is to pray in your heavenly language as much as possible.

"Likewise the Spirit also helps in our weaknesses. For we do not know what we should pray for as we ought, but the Spirit Himself makes intercession for us with groanings which

cannot be uttered. Now He who searches the hearts knows what the mind of the Spirit is, because He makes intercession for the saints according to the will of God." Romans 8:26-27

Praying in your heavenly language continually sets you up for your future as you are praying perfect prayers in the spirit. I want to encourage you to pray in tongues as much as you can throughout the day, and you will begin to notice how it's wonderfully affecting your life!

GOD WILL CONFIRM YOUR CALLING

Whatever it is that you are called to do in this life, I believe that Father God will confirm it for you to help guide you to where you need to go. He's a great big God, we are His little children, and He knows what we have to go through on this earth to fulfill our destinies.

Many times, God will give you a dream, a prophetic word by a trusted prophet, He will give you a sign that you have been looking for, a vision, wise counsel from someone who is spiritually mature and so on. Of course, He expects you to trust and obey Him no matter what, but I personally believe that if your heart is pure in the asking, that He will confirm your calling one way or another. He's a good Father. I also believe that if you believe God is telling you to go a certain direction with your calling, but you have actually misinterpreted or misunderstood what He said, if you remain humble and teachable, He will nudge you in the right direction. Again, keep your heart pure and in love with

Jesus, and you will keep heading towards your destiny.

WHO WILL GO?

I want to remind you that we are ALL called to *go* for God. Your "go" and my "go" are totally different, but we are all still called to go. Did you know that two-thirds of God's name is go? I believe that when we are all together in Heaven one day, we will get to share with each other about the things we were able to do for God on earth to bring Him glory. I am praying that you will very soon have a fresh encounter with God where you will know that you know like the prophet Isaiah what you're supposed to do:

"In the year that King Uzziah died, I saw the Lord sitting on a throne, high and lifted up, and the train of His robe filled the temple. Above it stood seraphim; each one had six wings: with two he covered his face, with two he covered his feet, and with two he flew. And one cried to another and said:

"Holy, holy, holy is the LORD of hosts; The whole earth is full of His glory!" And the posts of the door were shaken by the voice of him who cried out, and the house was filled with smoke. So I said: "Woe is me, for I am undone! Because I am a man of unclean lips, and I dwell in the midst of a people of unclean lips; For my eyes have seen the King, the LORD of hosts."

Then one of the seraphim flew to me, having in his hand a live coal which he had taken with the tongs from the altar.

And he touched my mouth with it, and said: "Behold, this has touched your lips; Your iniquity is taken away, and your sin purged."

Also I heard the voice of the Lord, saying: "Whom shall I send, and who will go for Us?" Then I said, "Here am I! Send me." Isaiah 6:1-8

Who is God going to send on His behalf? Will you follow God? Will you fulfill the destiny on your life? Isaiah was asked by God, who will go? I'm not sure if anybody else was standing there but Isaiah at that moment! But in this encounter, God wanted Isaiah *to want to go for Him*. How about you?

Beloved, here's the bottom line: as you stay close to God, worshipping Him, praying, fasting, living pure, denying yourself, studying His Word, serving and loving others and praying in your heavenly language, you WILL fulfill the call of God on your life. You will supernaturally step into your destiny, and no matter how hard the enemy tries, he cannot stop the call of God on your life! It won't always be easy, but in the end, it will all be worth it! One of the reasons why the enemy is trying to take you out is because of the unique, powerful and holy call on your life—no matter who you are. God is with you my friend!

"...I am with you always, even to the end of the age." Matthew 28:20

"Finally, there is laid up for me the crown of righteousness, which the Lord, the righteous Judge, will give to me on that Day, and not to me only but also to all who have loved His appearing." 2 Timothy 4:8

"God does not choose people because of their ability, but because of their availability." Brother Andrew

"Do all the good you can, by all the means you can, in all the ways you can, in all the places you can, at all the times you can, to all the people you can, as long as ever you can." John Wesley

KILLING LAZARUS

3

A MARY HEART

"To fall in love with God is the greatest of all romances; To seek Him, the greatest adventure; To find Him, the greatest of human achievement." Augustine

Did you know that we were never meant to leave the Garden of Eden?

"And they heard the sound of the LORD God walking in the garden in the cool of the day..." Genesis 3:8

In the Garden of Eden, Adam and Eve were clothed in glory and experienced daily fellowship with their Father. They enjoyed perfection in every way.

We were never meant to feel rejection, only the Father's love and acceptance of us. We were never meant to experience lust, only pure love. We were never meant to feel sickness, only divine health. We were never meant to have confusion, only peace. We were never meant to experience stress, anxiety, depression and fear, only joy.

We were created to never leave the Garden. The truest longing of our hearts is the glory of God in the midst of that garden life.

And as you know, what was once lost because of sin in the Garden, has been made new by the blood of Jesus. He brought us back to the Father, back into that right relationship with Him. And one day we will be with Him forever in Heaven. Right now, the Holy Spirit is within each believer, to guide us back to encounter the glory, peace, joy and love that was experienced in the Garden of Eden! Don't settle for the inferior pleasures of this world. Rather, seek the Lord with all of your heart, and you will encounter His indescribable presence in the midst of even the most ordinary moments of your day. Isn't that great news?

Lazarus knew this indescribable presence as he was one of the privileged ones that sat with Jesus and heard His beautiful words. Can you imagine what it must have been like to have sweet fellowship with the very Son of God? Lazarus was a friend of Jesus, and Jesus was a friend of Lazarus.

"Now Jesus loved Martha and her sister and Lazarus." John 11:5

There was something about this family that really pulled on the heartstrings of Jesus. He loved to spend time with them. I believe that one of those reasons was that they had a deeper revelation and understanding of who Jesus was than even some of the disciples at the time that He walked the earth. They simply loved and adored Jesus. And I believe that Jesus enjoyed spending time with them because He felt loved and embraced by this family with no strings attached.

Of all three, Martha, Mary and Lazarus, it's recorded that Mary had the most unique heart among them. Her heart was absolutely abandoned to the Master.

Another reason why the enemy is trying to take you out is to disrupt any and all intimacy you have with Jesus. The enemy is continually trying to come between you and Jesus. He is trying to do everything he can to keep you from the secret place of God (see Psalm 91). Why? Because he knows that the Secret Place of God is the most beautiful, sacred, intimate, rewarding place you can ever be in this life.

There are a number of different ways that the enemy is trying to prevent you from sweet communion with the Lord. He will try to get you to misunderstand God. He will try to get you to believe that God is not a good and loving Father. He will try to keep you busy with life. He will try to keep you stressed out, overwhelmed and full of anxiety. What happens is that the enemy will try to draw believers away from intimacy with God by looking to the world for immediate satisfaction or a quick fix that temporarily relieves them from life's pressures. He does this to deceive Christians and dull their senses which, in turn, hinders their communion with God. He will try to make you feel or think that God does not answer your prayers or that you are not loved by Father God. The enemy will try to entice you with worldly pleasures that temporarily satisfy but always leave you feeling empty and in shame. He uses shame along with lies to keep us from running back to a loving Father. He wants you to feel as though God is unwelcoming, distant and continually upset at you.

The enemy will also try to wound your heart or get you into offense, bitterness and unforgiveness so that your heart is hardened to the point where you avoid God altogether. All the while, Father God is longing to spend time with you and heal all the broken places. Are you beginning to see what's going on here? Beloved, you are not unloved or rejected by God. In fact, this is what He is doing right now over your life:

"The LORD your God in your midst, the Mighty One, will save; He will rejoice over you with gladness, He will quiet you with His love, He will rejoice over you with singing." Zephaniah 3:17

God *is* love, and He loves you with all of His heart. But the enemy doesn't want you to believe that. He's trying to take you out of that place of joyful intimacy with the Lord.

Friends, the enemy knows that the secret to lasting joy is found in the presence of God. There is no close second.

"You will show me the path of life; In Your presence is fullness of joy; At Your right hand are pleasures forevermore." Psalm 16:11

I have had the wonderful privilege of visiting Heaven on several occasions and have felt the indescribable euphoria that fills the air around you when you are there. I have felt that same atmosphere on earth on a few occasions when the glory of the Lord has come into the place where I was.

One of the times that I was in Heaven, I was able to feel all of the fruit of the Spirit flowing through me at 100% capacity, all at the same time. I felt 100% love, joy, peace, longsuffering, kindness, goodness, faithfulness, gentleness and self-control all at the same time (see Galatians 5). The one that stood out to me more than the others was peace. There is so much peace in your heart and mind in Heaven that it is literally impossible to worry or be confused in any way whatsoever. Beloved, this is our inheritance in the Lord. Why am I telling you this? Because if we pay the price of developing a life of prayer and intimate communion with Jesus, we will begin to encounter Heaven in our daily lives. Jesus told us to pray that:

"Your kingdom come. Your will be done on earth as it is in heaven." Matthew 6:10

And you are already seated in heavenly places with Christ:

"and raised us up together, and made us sit together in the heavenly places in Christ Jesus" Ephesians 2:6

We are already positioned to encounter and receive from God. Now, we must yield to Jesus and say no to those things that are trying to draw our hearts away from Him.

"Therefore submit to God. Resist the devil and he will flee from you. Draw near to God and He will draw near to you..." *James 4:7-8*

Mary, Lazarus' sister, knew what it was like to have a heart that was entirely in love with and devoted to Jesus:

"Then, six days before the Passover, Jesus came to Bethany, where Lazarus was who had been dead, whom He had raised from the dead. There they made Him a supper; and Martha served, but Lazarus was one of those who sat at the table with Him.

Then Mary took a pound of very costly oil of spikenard, anointed the feet of Jesus, and wiped His feet with her hair. And the house was filled with the fragrance of the oil.

But one of His disciples, Judas Iscariot, Simon's son, who would betray Him, said, "Why was this fragrant oil not sold for three hundred denarii and given to the poor?" This he said, not that he cared for the poor, but because he was a thief, and had the money box; and he used to take what was put in it.

But Jesus said, "Let her alone; she has kept this for the day of My burial. For the poor you have with you always, but Me you do not have always." John 12:1-8 (see also Matthew 26:6-13 and Mark 14:3-9)

Here we see that Jesus came to Bethany (approximately 1.5 miles from Jerusalem) six days before the Passover. Just six nights before He gave His life for all mankind, He spent those precious moments with those He loved: Mary, Martha, Lazarus and the disciples. Jesus could have been anywhere in these final moments of His life on earth, but He chose to spend them with His closest friends. Jesus loves to be close to His friends. And if you are born again, you are also His friend.

Every one of us has the same divine invitation to be a friend of God, and the enemy knows that. So, he is trying to do everything he can to separate us from sweet communion with God.

In our story with Mary of Bethany, there were a number of people that had gathered together to spend time with Jesus. I'm sure that Jesus' heart was already becoming heavy, knowing what He was about to suffer at the hands of the religious leaders. Being with His friends was comforting. Jesus had been repeatedly and intimately sharing with His disciples that He was soon going to die, and yet they remained distant and disconnected from what He was conveying to them. However, Mary's heart was responding uniquely different than everyone else in the room. She had a sense of what was about to take place and wanted to simply pour out her extravagant love to Jesus the only way she knew how.

The reason I like to share about Mary of Bethany is because

she was just like you and me. She wasn't one of the mighty apostles. There is no record of her casting out devils or healing the sick. She was not a prophetess or a teacher. No, she was ordinary, just like you and me. Jesus loves the "ordinary" ones...those who choose to simply love the Lord with all their hearts without having to be told or reminded to love. She loved simply and simply loved, and Jesus loved and adored her "ordinary heart".

Beloved, when we choose to love the Lord with all of our heart, mind, soul and strength, it touches the heart of God. He knows we have a choice to love. He knows we have a choice to what extremes we will go in our pursuit of loving Him.

Jesus is looking for that "one". That one heart in a room full of others that goes beyond ordinary love and devotion. Mary was an "ordinary" person, but demonstrated an extraordinary heart of love. And in the midst of her being simple and ordinary, she did something extravagant and extraordinary for Jesus.

The enemy is after your devotion to Jesus. That's one of the reasons he's trying to take you out. He does not want us in continual fellowship with God and will try to complicate our devotion to the Lord. In whatever ways he can wedge himself and his lies between us and God, he will try to do it. We have to daily resist those things that are trying to pull us away from intimacy.

Having a passionate and extraordinary heart for God is not measured by how big your ministry is. It's not measured by how many books you have written or how much money you make or how much influence you have. It's not measured by what you know—it's measured by Who you know and how well you know Him. A passionate, loving, extraordinary heart is measured by your devotion to sitting at the feet of Jesus, giving Him your love. We need a Mary heart...

Let that sink in.

Many Christians feel that they have to work and work towards this level of love and devotion to Jesus. The key to loving Jesus wholeheartedly is surrendering our hearts to Him every day. It's not about being godly enough or having enough time in the day or when all of your circumstances line up. No. It's about right now—this moment—no matter what is taking place in your life or what you've been through. This moment—surrender it to the Lord and things will begin to shift for you. Friends, this is a daily devotion. Not just when you feel like it or when you feel cornered because of the pressures of life.

Let me give you one of the greatest secrets of living the Christian life: Loving God with all your heart, enjoying His presence and surrendering to Him does not happen in the "spiritual" times of our lives—the so-called mountain top experiences (such as church services, prayer meetings, encounters with God, etc.) as much as in sitting at His feet, cultivating the thousands of "ordinary" moments every day.

Even the word ordinary sounds, well, ordinary. But that's the secret! The ordinary moments of life are where we spend most of our time.

Do you ever notice how the enemy seems to temporarily back off when you are at church, a prayer meeting or a Bible Study? That's because it's more difficult for him to come in and disrupt your heart when you are in those cooperate spiritual gatherings. Too many lovers of God and too many angels are in the room, and that makes demons nervous— they would rather wait outside for you to leave. Then you get back in your car to go home, and the enemy immediately tries to steal away from you what God did in a particular meeting. The secret is to keep going after God in your car, at your home, at your job, at your school or anywhere else. Just do what Heidi Baker told me once, "Never unplug from His presence, period!" I can tell you right now, the enemy does not know what to do with a Christian that has yielded their heart to God, worshipping Him and loving Him, in the ordinary moments of life.

I have felt the glory of God come on me so strong in my everyday life. In fact, as I am thinking about it right now, the most incredible experiences I have ever had with God, where I have felt His love, presence and glory manifest the strongest, were never in a corporate gathering with other believers. They were always spontaneous and in the most random of places. However, what was I doing prior to those random encounters? Thinking about Him. Worshipping Him.

Talking to Him. Loving Him. I love that, because you never know when God will visit you.

You too, can encounter the presence and glory of God in any of the ordinary moments of life. When we learn the secret of pursuing the heart of God at home, in the car, at work, at a coffee shop, on a hike, doing the dishes, mowing the lawn or anywhere else, we will find ourselves continually enjoying the presence of God, walking in His love, keeping all of our divine appointments, all the while giving the enemy a constant headache.

I know that you want this kind of supernatural lifestyle. I know that you want to love Jesus with your whole heart, but we become so easily distracted from it. The enemy wants to distract us from the simplicity of loving God with all of our hearts. The enemy wants to get us caught up in religion and religious activity that distracts us from sitting at His feet, gazing into His heart. He wants us to get caught up in the cares of this world and living under the pressures of this life. Remember what Jesus said to Mary's sister, Martha:

""...Martha, Martha, you are worried and troubled about many things. But one thing is needed, and Mary has chosen that good part, which will not be taken away from her." Luke 10:41-42

Are you "choosing" (because it's always a choice) the good part? Because if you are, it won't be taken away from you in this life or in the life to come. You see, we want to love, serve and give our whole hearts to Jesus out of love and devotion because we want to, not because we have to. But when we do seek Him with all of our hearts, everything changes!

"But seek first the kingdom of God and His righteousness, and all these things shall be added to you." Matthew 6:33

I'm afraid that most Christians are not seeking the Lord with all of their hearts, because they are not really sure what they are searching for.

"And you will seek Me and find Me, when you search for Me with all your heart." Jeremiah 29:13

Let's say that I came over to your home, sat your family down and told you that somewhere in your house I hid a brand new, crisp, $1 bill. This $1 bill could be hidden in the attic, under the floorboards, buried in the wall, embedded in the plumbing—it could be anywhere. Then I told you to seek out this $1 bill, and when you find it, it's yours...now go for it! What would your response be? You would probably say, "Thanks, but no thanks. I think we'll pass on that offer. We are not going to tear our house apart for one measly dollar." Why? Because searching for $1 is not worth all the trouble and effort it would take to find it.

Now let's take that same scenario, and instead of me telling you that there is $1 bill hidden in your house, I tell you that it's a check made out to your family in the amount of 10 million dollars. Again, it could be hidden anywhere. How would you respond? You would, of course, work day and night, 24/7 until you found that check. Why? Because of the incredible value of what you would find. You would seek that 10 million dollars with all of your heart, because you know what will happen when you find it.

It's the same with seeking the Lord with all of our hearts. If we don't think He's a good Father, or if we think nothing will ever happen when we pray, we are the "black sheep" of God's family, or that God doesn't love us, we will not go on searching for God with all of our heart, mind, soul and strength. And when we don't seek Him, we don't find Him. It's that simple.

If you would simply understand the great reward that comes to us when we search for God with all of our hearts, it will make any level of seeking Him entirely worth it.

"Finding God" is the greatest experience a person could ever have while on this earth. There is no close second. There is no price too great to pay to be close and stay close to Jesus. He is everything we need, desire and are looking for in this life.

"Again, the kingdom of heaven is like treasure hidden in a field, which a man found and hid; and for joy over it he goes and sells all that he has and buys that field. "Again, the kingdom of heaven is like a merchant seeking beautiful

pearls, who, when he had found one pearl of great price, went and sold all that he had and bought it." Matthew 13:44-46

Few things make the devil as nervous as Christians sitting continually at the feet Jesus.

You and I have this moment right now—whether it's a spiritual "mountain-top" moment or an "ordinary" moment—to sit at the feet of Jesus enjoying His heart. We still have breath, so we still have time. It's not too late to start, right now, practicing sitting at the feet of Jesus.

We lose the "freshness" and enjoyment of our love relationship with Jesus when we avoid the secret place of God. We all have to make the choice to stay renewed and refreshed in His presence by continually sitting with Jesus like Mary did.

The enemy may be trying to take you out by telling you that sitting at the feet of Jesus is not worth it. But you know that's a lie. He knows what will happen to you when you completely abandon yourself to the Lord. Don't lose heart, Jesus will do those things He promised He would do for you as you seek Him with all your heart.

Back to our story with Mary. Everyone was talking to one another, maybe finishing supper and listening to Jesus when all of a sudden, Mary came into the room where Jesus was reclining. She was boldly and proudly carrying her most valuable possession, a pound of very costly oil of spikenard (a very costly perfume).

Without a word, Mary pours this precious oil all over Jesus' head and feet, wiping His feet with her hair. Can you imagine the fragrance that must have filled the room? Always remember that wholehearted love for Jesus is a very beautiful fragrance to Him. Our hearts of love is the "perfume" that we can give and pour out on Jesus.

You can imagine that silence and shock are on the faces of everyone as the fragrance is filling the room. Everyone is looking at Jesus to see how He is going to respond to this "strange" act of love. There are hearts in the room that are judging both Jesus and Mary as this divine, intimate moment is taking place.

What was Jesus going to say about this? How was He going to respond to Mary? I'm sure that every heart in the room was wrestling with this whole scenario. Then, several people (it was not just Judas that complained as we see in Mark 14 and Matthew 26) spoke up about the "waste" that was just committed. They were upset with Mary! The people in the room could not understand what was going on in the precious heart of Mary.

Mary wasn't even paying attention to the stares, the complaining and the criticism from those in the room. People tend to criticize what they don't understand, especially those who are not living out of a heart of love for

God, but are going through the motions of Christianity. Isn't it just like the enemy the way the people responded to Mary? She simply loved Jesus with all of her heart, and it went against their religious protocol. We don't love Jesus in such a way to draw attention to ourselves; that's not what was going on here. Your love for God is not measured by your response to Him when people are watching, but how well you love each and every day when no one is watching. It's my opinion that Mary felt her heart was going to explode if she didn't do something in the natural that mirrored what was going on within her heart. I believe that she had a sense that Jesus was about to leave this earth, and she wanted to love and bless Him before He departed. In other words, Mary was saying, "Jesus, I know You are about to leave this world, so here's a token of my love for you to thank you for what you are about to do. Jesus, hold this moment in your heart as you are about to give your life for humanity." Mary gave Jesus something He could carry to the cross. Oh, what Jesus must have been feeling and thinking, "She gets Me, she really gets My heart".

No matter what was going on in the room, Mary was unmoved. She really didn't care what anyone thought of her. She was doing this before an audience of One. She was not trying to draw attention to herself; she was simply lost in His presence, boldly sharing this moment with Jesus. We need a Mary heart. Who cares what others think about the intensity of your love and devotion to God? When our hearts and motives are pure, the Lord sees what we are doing for Him, and He takes great delight in it.

Jesus is not demanding extravagant love from you. He wants you to want to be with Him. He paid a great price for you to draw near to Him. He loves you so deeply as you are His beloved son or daughter. Mary did this because she wanted to. By doing this, she was saying to Jesus, I really, really, really love You. The enemy has been trying to take you out so that you do not develop and strengthen your love and intimacy for Jesus. You see, when we are passionately in love with Jesus, we become irresistible to Him, and that's when the enemy really begins to back off from us. There is a price to pay, yes. It was very costly what Mary gave to Jesus. When we have passion for Jesus, our hearts are ignited in such a way that we are looking within to see what fragrant offering we have to pour out to Him. And Mary knew it was "now or never"; she knew that this was her moment to pour over Jesus her devotion, to honor Him, to love Him and to declare His worth.

This is very difficult for me to say, but many Christians are not passionately in love with Jesus. That doesn't mean that they are in sin; they just don't know how to love Him passionately. Why? Because the enemy has gotten in somewhere and has disrupted their walk with God to the point that they have forgotten what really matters most—Jesus, 24/7.

Finally, Jesus spoke up and said, "Leave her alone". I love that. The people in the room were discerning the entire situation incorrectly.

Now, as we close out this chapter, this is one of my favorite parts of the story. The result of Mary pouring out this costly oil is that the perfume got on both Jesus *and* Mary. And for the next couple of days, everywhere that Jesus went, He had this fragrance on Him, and everywhere that Mary went, she had the same fragrance on her! Did you catch it? When the people around Jesus smelled the fragrance, they thought of Mary. When the people were around Mary, they thought of Jesus! The fragrance was on both of them. This is true intimacy. This is divine communion. This is love. This was the heart of Mary.

"Now when they saw the boldness of Peter and John, and perceived that they were uneducated and untrained men, they marveled. And they realized that they had been with Jesus." Acts 4:13

Beloved, when we have been with Jesus, we become like Him in our words, thoughts and actions, and people take notice of that. So does the enemy.

"And the evil spirit answered and said, '"Jesus I know, and Paul I know; but who are you?"' Acts 19:15

When we develop and cultivate a Mary-like heart, the enemy's plans are continually frustrated as he knows he can't win against a Christian who is deeply in love with Jesus.

There are infinite possibilities that can happen when we

cultivate a lifestyle of sitting at the feet of Jesus. I have listed for you just some of the *benefits and blessings* that we can experience when sitting at His feet (I personalized them for you):

It's a place where I can always go.

It does not matter the time, space or place.

I am always welcome there.

I am never too ugly, fat, skinny or dirty to be welcome.

My Father is always there.

It's where my sadness is turned to joy.

All my sins are forgiven.

It's a place of rest.

My strongholds are destroyed.

It's where answers are given.

It's where I lay down my burdens and pick up His.

It's where my heart is healed.

My past is not only forgiven, but forgotten.

I am never alone there.

I can laugh there.

I can dance there.

I can sing there, and no one ever cares that I am out of tune.

It's where the crooked places are made straight and the rough places are made smooth.

The cares of the world seem to melt away.

I can share my heart and never ever feel ashamed or embarrassed.

At His feet, I am allowed to share my deepest feelings.

I can cry at His feet.

I can spend hours and hours there or maybe just five minutes.

I always feel stronger and happier when I leave.

Demons cannot dwell there.

I can get lost there—for hours.

Time stands still.

Life can wait until I am through spending time at His feet.

Worry and confusion are not allowed entrance.

Love surrounds me.

I am not condemned there, though I may be gently reminded of things that need to change.

I can be myself.

I take off the cloak of heaviness and put on the garment of praise.

I am continually reminded of God's precious promises.

He reminds me there that everything in His Word is for me.

I can talk about others there and pray for them and not feel like I am gossiping.

I feel so protected there.

It's such a wonderful place of peace and rest for my soul.

We talk about our future plans together.

It's a place of worship and praise.

Jesus can't wait until I get there.

It's where I am filled to overflowing with the presence of God.

I can let down my guard.

It's where I can receive my orders for the day or plans for my future.

I can get my peace back.

I do not have to pretend there; I can always be real.

It's where I can pull up to the table of the Lord, and all of Heaven meets me there.

Every time I sit at His feet, I leave changed.

I come out lighter every time, because more of the flesh has died.

I am fed there with the Bread of Heaven.

I can take communion with Jesus.

He always reminds me that I am His special child.

It's where my mind is renewed.

It's where my soul is refreshed.

It's where my spirit is strengthened.

It's where my heart is ignited with His fire.

It's a place that even though I may not "feel" anything at times, I know that He is always there with me.

I am challenged there.

I make fresh commitments there and not empty promises.

I can rest in the loving arms of Jesus there.

He does not call me servant there, but friend.

I can unashamedly abandon myself to Him there.

I can hear His loving voice there.

I feel like I am the only one in the world that He is paying attention to right now, because He makes me feel welcome and secure.

All my tears are wiped away.

My heart seems to always be stronger for Him when I leave.

When I am at His feet, I know that everything is going to be alright.

No one but us understands what takes place there.

I fall in love with Jesus more every time.

I am never too busy to sit at His feet.

Though I may fail at times, I am never looked at as a failure there.

Leaving this place with Jesus puts such a longing in my heart for my next visit there.

It's a place that I am pursuing to live in every moment of every day.

It's where I can soar on eagles' wings.

It's where the Holy Spirit teaches me the wonderful things of God.

I have a new love for people when I leave there.

I am led beside still waters, green meadows and gardens of love there.

I receive a glimpse of Heaven there.

He always sees me as beautiful.

He always knows the right thing to say to my heart.

I never have to prove myself to Him there.

No earthly desire or pleasure compares to spending even one moment at His feet.

My heart is free there.

When I am sitting at His feet, I am not hiding from life's problems, but simply seeing them through His eyes.

When all hell seems to be breaking loose in my life, He reminds me that I am going to make it, because He is my strength.

I am humbled at His feet, because I see the real me.

I can be cleansed from the filth of the world there because of His precious Blood.

It's my get-a-way even when I can't get away.

It's a place to rest my mind, body, soul and spirit.

His grace surrounds me there.

His power flows through me there.

When I am at His feet, He shows me new areas to overcome but reminds me that He is always there to help.

He is my Beloved there.

He heals my deepest wounds at His feet.

Nothing I say to Him ever takes Him by surprise, because He is familiar with all my ways.

His banner over me is love.

He is always waiting for me there and looks forward to when I return.

I can let my heart be free in worship and praise to Him there.

He reminds me to lift my head up, because where I am weak, He is strong.

The only thing holding me back from daily spending time at His feet is me.

He reminds me to guard what He has entrusted to me there.

I have no past there.

He reminds me that the greatest way to approach Him is not in fear or shame, but as a little child.

After I have sat at His feet, I have a better understanding of what things grieve His heart and what things bring Him joy.

He is never too busy to welcome me to sit at His feet.

The more time I spend with Jesus, the more time I want to spend with Him.

I cast all my cares on Him there.

It's where feelings are never an indicator of His nearness, because He is always near to me—always.

It's such a gentle, quiet and peaceful place.

Jesus is proud of me there.

He loves me more than I will ever know!

Do you now see the wonderful, infinite possibilities that are found in Him when we sit at His feet? Everything changes when we develop a heart like Mary. When we sit at His feet and engage the Lord, there is no power in hell that can come against that sacred place. The beautiful thing we have to remember is that we carry Jesus within us. Therefore, we can "sit at His feet" anytime, anywhere, and the enemy can do absolutely nothing about it.

Beloved, get into the habit of sitting at His feet every day even if it's just for five minutes. The more we do this, the more we encounter His love, peace, power, joy, presence, etc., on a regular basis. Resist all the ways the enemy is trying to keep you from sitting at His feet. Again, the enemy knows what will happen to you and what will happen to him if you daily embrace a heart like Mary.

"The love of Christ both wounds and heals, it fascinates and frightens, it kills and makes alive, it draws and repulses. There can be nothing more terrible or wonderful than to be stricken with love for Christ so deeply that the whole being goes out in a pained adoration of His person, an adoration that disturbs and disconcerts while it purges and satisfies and relaxes the deep inner heart." A. W. Tozer

4

SONS AND DAUGHTERS

"You will treat yourself and others according to the way you think God feels about you." Jack Frost

A few years ago, I had dream that dozens of young people were very giddy and taking turns diving into a nasty open sewer. In the dream, the sewer represented the emptiness that the things of this world had to offer. Nevertheless, these young people were carefree and oblivious to what they were doing. I will never forget the look on a particular young girl's face once she came out of the sewer. She felt such shame, depression, hopelessness and ugliness. I know I will meet that girl one day; it was that clear in the dream. Anyway, she was looking to be clean. She knew she had made a mistake. She now realized this world had nothing for her. She was deceived by her friends. Beloved, just like you, she was made in the image of God.

Our beloved Lazarus was also made in the very image of God. The enemy hates that. He hates the fact that you were made in God's very own image and likeness.

"Then God said, '"Let Us make man in Our image, according to Our likeness...' So God created man in His own image; in the image of God He created him; male and female He created them." Genesis 1:26-27

It is absolutely essential that *you* understand (because the enemy already knows, but doesn't want *you* to ever know) how precious you are to Father God. You are His son. You are His daughter. Before the foundations of the world were laid, He was thinking about you—about your life. He had thoughts and plans of who you were going to become and what you were going to accomplish on this earth.

"Your eyes saw my substance, being yet unformed. And in your book they all were written, the days fashioned for me, when as yet there were none of them." Psalm 139:16

Another reason why the enemy is trying to take you out is because you are God's son or daughter. You are a child of God. The enemy has been trying to get you to misunderstand, complicate and devalue who you are in Christ.

From some, the enemy has even tried to bring gender confusion into your life. Just know that you were born the gender that God wanted you to be. God never makes a mistake. You are not a mistake no matter how you came into this world. The surrounding circumstances of your birth and upbringing may have contributed to your broken heart and the confusion that you feel on the inside, and the enemy has tried to exploit that. Always remember that Father's love for you is stronger than anything that anyone has ever said or done to you. Father God deeply loves you!

There is more freedom in being who God created you to be than you could ever imagine. When and where did we start learning to be something other than who God created us to be? For many, it started when they were young. There was some way about them that others didn't like or appreciate, and it caused them to emotionally retreat on the inside. When this happens over and over, by the time we become teenagers and then adults and have suppressed years of being ourselves, we inadvertently develop into someone other than God's original intent for our lives. It's still there, of course, but it's buried under the weight of how we feel about ourselves and what others have said and done to us.

This emotional wounding is keeping many believers from receiving Father's love, joy, and adoration over them. It also keeps them from accomplishing the great purpose for their lives that God has ordained for them before the foundation of the world. Instead of living healed and whole on the inside, they end up living a life that is far below a son or daughter of Father God.

Here are five ways that you can continue to *be someone that you're not:*

1. **You can completely disregard the uniqueness of who you are.** There's no one else like you. You are entirely different than the over 7 1/2 billion people in the world. Why would you want to be someone that you're not? There has never been another you, and there will never be another you. Before God even made the universe, He thought of you. He has loved you forever. We are literally made in the image of God, and we have to understand how powerful that is. Ask God for the revelation of His heart for you, and say, "Father, show me who I am. Reveal to me the wonderful thoughts that you have towards me. Forgive me for being someone that I am not, and restore my heart."

2. **Continue to live under the pressure of creating a social media presence that is longing for the attention of others.** It's seems as if some people's social media presence is one that is perpetually staged for someone to come and buy their house. Why are you so pressured to keep up appearances? It's certainly not Father's heart for you to live under the constant pressure of your social media presence. Have fun with social media, but don't let it own you, control you or make you out to be someone that you're not. To continually do that is a sign of a wounded heart that fears being rejected. Not everyone is going to like your style. What would happen to your emotions if someone criticized your, "Martha Stewart" type post? If you are not secure in His heart for you first and foremost, you will risk being devasted over someone's superficial response to your post or picture on social media.

3. **Compare yourself to others.** So what if you have a big nose or ugly feet or a bunch of wrinkles? You're going to continue to wound your heart by comparing your looks with others. You are who you are. Father loves all the shapes and sizes He created. Because you are wounded, you don't see yourself the way God sees you. Beauty is in the eye of the Beholder, and you are the one that Father is beholding—therefore you are beautiful. Again, you are made in His image. To make it plain, when we truly receive His love for us, we don't think this way any longer. We receive His love; it goes deep into us and heals and roots out any lie that the enemy tried to sow in us at any point in our lives. You are His beloved! You might as well start believing it!

4. **Go through the motions of being a Christian**. If you are going to call yourself a Christian, you might as well start living like it. Don't try to be someone that you are not. You are either an authentic Christian that follows Jesus or you're not. I have found it so fascinating how some Christians' theology will change after they go through something. Rather than forgiving and allowing God to heal their hearts, they develop new theology to accommodate the pain, trauma, disappointment and bitterness. Christianity is all about loving and serving Jesus wholeheartedly—nothing held back, no games, just completely in love with Jesus and willing to do whatever it takes to stay close to His heart. You need to be healed of whatever has separated you from the presence and power of God flowing through your life. He loves you dearly, but He wants ALL of you. Not the religious

you; the real you.

5. **Pretend.** Pretend to be happy. Pretend to not be hurt. Pretend that your marriage is not falling apart. Pretend that you can make ends meet. You can pretend, or you can get help. You can reach out to someone that will love you, pray you through and help you get healed. You can call out to God right now and ask Him to heal your broken heart. You have to come to the place where you're tired of living in your own strength. Friends, you can't do this life on your own. You need the Holy Spirit. You need people around you that love you and value you. Stop pretending to be ok. You need help, and Father is waiting with open arms to pull you in close and love you and heal you. It doesn't have to take years and years. You can be forgiven, cleansed and healed in a moment. He's a good Father, and He loves you and believes in you. Your future is bright! Submit to His heart. Draw near to Him, and He will make ALL things new!

You are incredibly loved! Everything is about to change for the better in your life as you yield to the Holy Spirit! As you bring all of this to the Lord, I'm believing that you will feel completely different even as you wake up tomorrow morning!

You see, when we really begin to tap into who we are in Christ, that's when we really become alive. We want to live so free within our hearts, knowing how much Father delights in us and enjoys us every day. Father doesn't *just* love you; He enjoys you!

He loves your uniqueness. He loves your personality. He enjoys watching you enjoy those things that He created for you to enjoy. He even puts things in your path that are meant to give you joy because He knows how much you enjoy them.

We must come to the place within our hearts that we believe and receive the truth that Father really does love us, believe in us and enjoy us as His sons and daughters. But for many, it's hard to come to that revelation because our hearts and minds are trying to war against the truth of how God feels about us. That war that you feel within has been one of satan's strategies from the very beginning to cause you to not trust Father's love for you.

How do you define your value, worth and beauty? If you don't define these things by Father's standard, then you have robbed yourself of the joy of living free as His beloved child. There are many believers out there that truly love the Lord, but are hanging on to a false identity about themselves.

There is a vast difference between who we were, who we are and who we will become! Every day as we draw closer to Him, any roadblocks and barriers, wounds and hurts, pains and disappointments melt away in the presence of His love.

You see, the story of your life is still being written. Whatever age you are now, that's the chapter you are in. Let's say you are 50 years old and you're going to live to be 95. Right now, you are in "Chapter 50" of your life. There are 45 more chapters to go! That's a lot of chapters left in your life. The book is still being written about you. Your story is not yet complete. You may have chapters in your life that have a divorce, a miscarriage or a bad mistake written into it, but those chapters don't define your whole story. As I said, the story is still being written. The enemy wants you to stay focused on what is contained in the past chapters (more on that later), but Father wants you stay focused on His love for you and the privilege of being one of his sons or daughters. Choose to not let the enemy hijack your identity any longer!

Your upbringing does not define you. Things that have happened to you do not define you. Your finances (how much you have or do not have) does not define you. Your job, how you look, your sickness and pain, how many friends you have, your grades, what your spouse thinks about you, how clean your house is, how anointed you are, how much talent you have, etc., does not define you. What defines you is what the Father thinks and feels about you. Jesus loves you just as much as He loved Lazarus. You belong at the same table with them.

"He brought me to the banqueting house, and his banner over me was love." Song of Solomon 2:4

His banner over you is, and will always be, love. He loves you and believes in you like nobody else does. He knows every struggle, heartache, pain and any other issues you may be facing, but Father still boldly declares His love and joy over you!

Your identity as a son or daughter is rooted in Father's opinion of you and not what others think of you, always remember that. Everyone seems to have an opinion of others, and most of those opinions are not the same as God's opinion of that same person.

Here's how we tend to think: We think that if others had the same knowledge about us that God does, we feel they would reject us, so we feel that Father will do the same. But He is all-consuming love! He believes in every one of us. We cannot let the opinions of others drown out the beautiful and wonderful thoughts that God has for each of us. The enemy will use people to try to get to you by attacking your identity.

WORDS OF LOVE

Always remember that if you want to know what God thinks about you, the Word of God is full of His Words of love to you. The Bible is really Father's love letter to His children. We also hear and receive His thoughts towards us by spending quality time with Him. Spending time in the Word and in intimate prayer with God strengthens and anchors our hearts to our true identity and not what the enemy would whisper to us.

This is why we must speak words of life to each other. Our

words are more powerful than we will ever realize.

"Death and life are in the power of the tongue, and those who love it will eat its fruit." Proverbs 18:21

"But I say to you that for every idle word men may speak, they will give account of it in the day of judgment." Matthew 12:36

We want to be known for speaking life to those around us. Even what may seem like a joke to you can hurt someone else because they are struggling with their identity. We don't want to pile on more hurt to an already wounded heart. That person standing before you is also a son or daughter of God. That makes them your brother or sister in the Lord.

The enemy never wants you to discover who you really are in Christ. He's afraid of that. He's afraid that you will live in the confidence of the Father's love towards you. I am convinced that when our hearts are truly awakened to how Father really sees us and how He really feels about us— that's when we really start to live. We are supposed to be living daily from the thoughts that Father God has towards us. Do we have weaknesses and shortcomings? Yes, we all do. However, those things do not define our walk with God.

YOU ARE A MASTERPIECE

"For we are His workmanship, created in Christ Jesus for good works, which God prepared beforehand that we should

walk in them." Ephesians 2:10

You are the created masterpiece of God! When He looks at you, He already sees a finished work of art. And although we don't yet fully see what He sees or have the full revelation like we ought to, as we open our hearts to God and receive, each day becomes a fresh unveiling of His heart towards you.

Unfortunately, many believers do not see themselves as the beautiful artwork of God. They are just trying to get through another day unscathed by life's problems and demands. But the Lord wants us to live out of the reality of belonging to Him as His sons and daughters.

YOU ARE LOVED

Father God really, really loves you! No matter what emotions that last sentence brings up within you, it doesn't change the fact that you are deeply loved and adored by Father God. He loves you with a joyful, deep and everlasting love.

"...Yes, I have loved you with an everlasting love; Therefore with lovingkindness I have drawn you." Jeremiah 31:3

Here's the problem: It's one thing to talk about Father's love, yet it's an entirely different thing to live loved—to live daily feeling the sweet and strong embrace of Abba's love.

"And because you are sons, God has sent forth the Spirit of

His Son into your hearts, crying out, '"Abba, Father!"'
Galatians 4:6

Beloved, you belong to Abba. You are not an orphan; you are a son or daughter. Quit listening to the lies of the enemy, and live in the revelation that Father loves, desires, adores and enjoys you each and every day.

I will never forget looking out of my second story window watching my son run around in the backyard laughing and playing with his friends when he was little. As I was watching him, I heard the voice of the Lord say this to me, "See? At this moment, you don't remember a single thing your son has ever done wrong. You are enjoying him as you watch him laugh and play. It's the same with Me. When you ask me to forgive you, I don't remember anything wrong you have done. I look at you with love and joy." That really touched my heart.

The problem that I find with many, many Christians is that they do not know how to live like a son or daughter. Instead they are living as an orphan with an orphan spirit. So many believers are living with a wounded heart which manifests itself in a spirit of rejection.

A ROOT OF REJECTION

Rejection manifests itself in many forms such as being passed over for a promotion, rejected by someone you wanted to go on a date with, rejected because you are a

Christian, maybe someone made fun of the way you looked, or maybe you were not good at sports. Maybe you feel rejected because other moms "seem" to have their act together, and you do not. Maybe you feel like your ideas or opinions are always rejected. Maybe you have never been able to make friends easily. Maybe you're not very handy with tools, and others make fun of you. Maybe someone you thought was a friend gossiped about you. And the list goes on and on.

For some, rejection is more than an occasional manifestation. It's a struggle throughout their entire lives, deeply rooted and intertwined into their identities since they were a child. And the enemy tries to exploit these deep roots by making people think that Father God has also rejected them their entire life, and nothing could be farther from the truth.

A root of rejection can manifest itself in many different ways such as pride, lust, low self-esteem, overeating, laziness, depression, false humility, striving, anger, always trying to please people, etc. When we receive healing from all that has wounded us and replace the enemy's lies with the truth of what God thinks and feels about us, our entire life changes. When we are healed, we change so dramatically that our personalities even change, our interaction with those closest to us changes, how we interact with the world around us changes, and best yet, our relationship with God changes. When we are healed from an orphan spirit, we experience Father God in a whole new way. He will no longer seem like a distant, untouchable, angry, sad Father. Rather, you will see that everything Father God says and does is because of His love for you, even when He disciplines you.

"And you have forgotten the exhortation which speaks to you as to sons: '"My son, do not despise the chastening of the LORD, nor be discouraged when you are rebuked by Him; For whom the LORD loves He chastens, and scourges every son whom He receives."' If you endure chastening, God deals with you as with sons; for what son is there whom a father does not chasten? But if you are without chastening, of which all have become partakers, then you are illegitimate and not sons. Furthermore, we have had human fathers who corrected us, and we paid them respect. Shall we not much more readily be in subjection to the Father of spirits and live?" Hebrews 12:5-9

I know that your heart is being stirred and awakened even now to live loved! However, if you are reading this and say, "This is great revelation!", I want to lovingly tell you that revelation doesn't change you. It's what you do with the revelation that changes you. You must walk this out every day, because the enemy is trying to take you out with those things that are opposite of Father's heart for you.

The other day, I saw a short video that really impacted me. It showed two kids (maybe around 12 years old) sitting together at a fine restaurant. I'm paraphrasing here, but the boy says to the girl, "I just saw the prettiest girl I have ever seen!" He tells her to look slowly to her left. As she curiously turns her head, she sees herself in the mirror, and the look on her face is worth all the gold in the world! Friends, Father God, really, really, really loves you! You're His favorite!

"The LORD your God in your midst, the Mighty One, will save; He will rejoice over you with gladness, He will quiet you with His love, He will rejoice over you with singing." Zephaniah 3:17

This is one of my favorite verses in the Bible. Father God (of the Old Testament, by the way!) is with you right now. He is so happy and excited about you. He is rejoicing over you with singing. He has written a song about you! He has a glad heart towards you. Receive that truth within the deepest place in your heart. Meditate on this verse in Zephaniah until it becomes part of you. The enemy will try to tell you (even now) that that's not how He feels about you—that's a lie. It's in the Word of God; therefore, it's absolute. You have not gone so far that His love can't reach you.

"For as many as are led by the Spirit of God, these are sons of God. For you did not receive the spirit of bondage again to fear, but you received the Spirit of adoption by whom we cry out, '"Abba, Father."' The Spirit Himself bears witness with our spirit that we are children of God, and if children, then heirs—heirs of God and joint heirs with Christ, if indeed we suffer with Him, that we may also be glorified together." Romans 8:14-17

You are not a slave; you are a son or daughter of God. It is one of the enemy's favorite deceptions to make you feel less than loved as Father God's child. He knows you're saved, but he will do all that he can to make you feel distant from God like a slave with no rights, privileges or love. And that binds our hearts so that we are not able to receive and give love to our wonderful Father. And when we do not have a healthy view of Father God, we will live feeling that we are continually falling short of Father loving us with all of His heart.

MEPHIBOSHETH

As we close this chapter, I want to share with you a powerful story from the life of David. The King's heart towards Mephibosheth is a type of how Jesus welcomes each one of us (like Lazarus) to sit at His table.

"Jonathan, Saul's son, had a son who was lame in his feet. He was five years old when the news about Saul and Jonathan came from Jezreel; and his nurse took him up and fled. And it happened, as she made haste to flee, that he fell and became lame. His name was Mephibosheth." 2 Samuel 4:4

"Now David said, '"Is there still anyone who is left of the house of Saul, that I may show him kindness for Jonathan's sake?"' And there was a servant of the house of Saul whose name was Ziba. So when they had called him to David, the king said to him, '"Are you Ziba?"' He said, '"At your

service!"' Then the king said, '"Is there not still someone of the house of Saul, to whom I may show the kindness of God?"' And Ziba said to the king, '"There is still a son of Jonathan who is lame in his feet."' So the king said to him, '"Where is he?"' And Ziba said to the king, '"Indeed he is in the house of Machir the son of Ammiel, in Lo Debar."'

Then King David sent and brought him out of the house of Machir the son of Ammiel, from Lo Debar. Now when Mephibosheth the son of Jonathan, the son of Saul, had come to David, he fell on his face and prostrated himself.

Then David said, '"Mephibosheth?"' And he answered, '"Here is your servant!"' So David said to him, '"Do not fear, for I will surely show you kindness for Jonathan your father's sake, and will restore to you all the land of Saul your grandfather; and you shall eat bread at my table continually."'

Then he bowed himself, and said, '"What is your servant, that you should look upon such a dead dog as I?"' And the king called to Ziba, Saul's servant, and said to him, '"I have given to your master's son all that belonged to Saul and to all his house. You therefore, and your sons and your servants, shall work the land for him, and you shall bring in the harvest, that your master's son may have food to eat. But Mephibosheth your master's son shall eat bread at my table always."'

Now Ziba had fifteen sons and twenty servants. Then Ziba

said to the king, '"According to all that my lord the king has commanded his servant, so will your servant do."' '"As for Mephibosheth,"' said the king, '"he shall eat at my table like one of the king's sons."' Mephibosheth had a young son whose name was Micha. And all who dwelt in the house of Ziba were servants of Mephibosheth. So Mephibosheth dwelt in Jerusalem, for he ate continually at the king's table. And he was lame in both his feet." II Samuel 9:1-13

What a powerful story. King David made the first move to rescue Mephibosheth, I love that. As a church, and as Christians, we are to help others the same way.

"Then He also said to him who invited Him, '"When you give a dinner or a supper, do not ask your friends, your brothers, your relatives, nor rich neighbors, lest they also invite you back, and you be repaid. But when you give a feast, invite the poor, the maimed, the lame, the blind. And you will be blessed, because they cannot repay you; for you shall be repaid at the resurrection of the just."'" Luke 14:12-14

Start getting into the habit of blessing and ministering to people that can't pay you back. There are so many hurting and broken people, both inside and outside the church.

Mephibosheth was only five years old when his father died in battle and he became crippled. He was now about twenty-one years old and had a young son of his own. The crippling that happened to Mephibosheth was not even his fault. What did Mephibosheth feel like on the inside?

How would you have felt on the inside? Maybe you'd wonder if anyone loved you just the way you were. Maybe you thought, "God how can you love me? Have you seen my weakness? Have you seen my feet? Look at me, I have nothing to offer. I'm a mess! My heart is a mess."

Not too long ago, someone called me with those very words saying, "I'm a mess, and I have made a mess out of my life." The conversation I had with this person reminds me of this story. We get so focused on our weakness, our emotional deformities, our brokenness, our shame or our past, when in fact, we are called to sit at the King's table. And not just sit at the King's table, but enjoy the rights and privileges as a son or daughter of the King.

Remember that you are made in the image and likeness of God, and you were created for the Garden of Eden and to live in His presence 24/7. This is what the enemy is trying to keep us from every day. The enemy doesn't want us to figure out who we really are, why we are really here and what God has for us in this life and in the life to come.

The enemy doesn't want you to figure out that you are a son or daughter of God. Then enemy wants you to constantly "look at your feet" and feel hopeless, unlovely and discouraged. You will never feel comfortable sitting at the table with Jesus when you live out of a place of shame. His love is so deep and so perfect that it's hard to believe that He receives us when we feel like such a mess.

In the natural, Mephibosheth could not give anything to David. He had no real usefulness to David and only could offer him love, loyalty and thankfulness. And that's where we start. That's where things begin to shift for broken and wounded people.

Who was around David's table? His own sons and men of great honor. I am sure others were jealous of Mephibosheth saying, "Why does he deserve this? Have you seen his feet? Have you seen his weakness?" Mephibosheth ends up getting totally blessed and highly favored by the king in front of everyone. What an undeserved honor to be so close to the king continually as one of the king's sons! Don't you love that?

"...he shall eat at my table like one of the king's sons." 2 Samuel 9:11

In essence, King David was saying that Mephibosheth would not be treated like anything but a son! Now, under the kings table, Mephibosheth's lame feet were still there, but that made no difference to King David. He loved, cared for, blessed and favored him regardless. Oh, what Mephibosheth's heart must have felt like so loved, blessed and cared for as everything was restored to him.

Father God's desire for you is the restoration of all that has been lost emotionally, physically, financially and spiritually. You *are* one of the King's sons or daughters with all the rights and privileges of a child of God. Mephibosheth's identity was no longer in his deformity, but in sonship.

By the way, the name Mephibosheth means "dispeller, or one who drives away shame".

A few years ago, I was at my niece's high school graduation. I think there was about three thousand people in attendance including the students. At the beginning of the ceremony, someone made an announcement about everyone in the audience holding applause and cheers until the end so they can quickly get through all the names of those graduating. I will never forget as long as I live what happened next. About a third of the way through the ceremony, one of the graduating student's name was called, and from the other side of the auditorium a father yelled out, "THAT'S MY BOY!" It was so loud and clear and heartfelt. It touched me deeply. What a proud dad! It brings tears to my eyes reliving the moment in my heart as I write this story.

Father God feels the same way about you as He looks your way. He says, "That's my boy! That's my girl!". You have captured the heart of God, my friends. You are His sons and daughters. Don't ever let the enemy tell you anything different!

"My deepest awareness of myself is that I am deeply loved by Jesus Christ, and I have done nothing to earn it or deserve it." Brennan Manning

5

THE BATTLE FOR YOUR TESTIMONY

"If you take a stand [for God] and mean it, you may suffer persecution. Some of your friends will drift away. They don't want to be with people like you. You speak to their conscience. They feel uncomfortable in your presence because you lived for God." Billy Graham

Did you know that anyone you cross paths with at any given moment can be affected by your life? You are a living testimony of the goodness of God.

"You are our epistle written in our hearts, known and read by all men." 2 Corinthians 3:2

Your life is a testimony of God's faithfulness, love, deliverance, healing, salvation, power and everything else that God has done for you. You can make a difference in the life of so many others because of what Jesus has done in you. You should be proud to say to people, "Look what the Lord has done!"

TESTIMONY TIME!

"And they overcame him by the blood of the Lamb and by the word of their testimony, and they did not love their lives to the death." Revelation 12:11

One of the main reasons why the chief priests wanted to kill Lazarus was because many of the Jews were turning their hearts to Jesus on account of Lazarus being raised from the dead.

"Now a great many of the Jews knew that He was there; and they came, not for Jesus' sake only, but that they might also see Lazarus, whom He had raised from the dead. But the chief priests plotted to put Lazarus to death also, because on account of him many of the Jews went away and believed in Jesus." John 12:9-11

For as long as Lazarus lived after being raised from the dead, he was a thorn in the side of the religious leaders and skeptics of his day. Everywhere that Lazarus went, he was literally a walking testimony. That's why they hated him. The chief priests and others wanted him dead, because his life continually gave glory to Jesus. How could they deny or discredit what happened to Lazarus? Everyone knew he was raised from the dead by Jesus.

I love how this Scripture says that many believed in Jesus because of Lazarus. Isn't that what this life is all about? Pointing people to Jesus? You see, the enemy does not want your life to point others to Jesus in any way whatsoever. If you are born-again, you have a testimony. It doesn't matter if you were saved at five years old and grew up in church your whole life or you got saved last week from decades of drug and alcohol abuse; you have a testimony.

I have heard people say over the years that they don't have much of a testimony. What? Are you kidding me? No matter when or how you became born again, you have gone from darkness to light on the inside. Your destiny is not Hell, but Heaven!

"For you were once darkness, but now you are light in the Lord. Walk as children of light." Ephesians 5:8

It's a very powerful testimony to have been born again at a young age and to have grown up in church all your life and not ever have handed yourself over to the world. That's a very powerful testimony that the Lord cherishes deeply and the enemy hates.

On the other hand, you may have lived for the world a good portion of your life and have not been born again that long. That too, is a very powerful testimony—that in the midst of being full of the world and wickedness, you chose to say, "Enough is enough. I need Jesus." The enemy hates this testimony as well.

No matter what your testimony is (again, all who are born again have one), one of the things that the enemy fears the most is that you are going to share with others the good things the Lord has done for you. And the enemy does not just fear your salvation testimony. He also fears that you will share with others about all the wonderful things that God has done for you *since* you have been born again—how God has healed you, set you free, performed miracles on your behalf, saved lost loved ones, blessed you beyond measure and how He walks and talks with you every day!

We want to get to a place in God where the enemy fears that we even woke up this morning! We want the enemy to say, "Oh no! She's up!" We want the enemy to fear that we simply walked into the grocery store and say, "Look who's coming! Run!"

"The wicked flee when no one pursues, but the righteous are bold as a lion." Proverbs 28:1

Did you know that when you love the Lord, are yielded to the Spirit and are on fire for God, the enemy is afraid that at any moment you could share with someone about Jesus? This makes the enemy very, very uncomfortable. The enemy knows that angels are assigned to help you bring the Kingdom of Heaven wherever you go (this is the premise of my book, *Carrying the Presence*), so he does everything he can to not let that happen.

"...For indeed, the kingdom of God is within you." Luke 17:21

The other day, I was at the local grocery store grabbing a slice of pizza to go. I was simply waiting for the young lady to finish heating up my pizza when the Holy Spirit whispered to me that this lady was a first responder. I shrugged it off because she was fixing my pizza and it didn't make sense to my natural mind. As I walked away, the glory of the Lord came all over me, and I knew I had to go back and talk to her. You may say, what does that mean, "the glory of the Lord came all over me?" Well, as I walked away, with pizza in hand, I could hardly stand because God's presence was so strong on me, and the atmosphere around me shifted completely. It felt as if I was in another realm.

So, I thought to myself, even if I am wrong, I can share Father's love for her. I walked back up to the counter, and I said, "Can I ask you a question?" she said yes. I said, "Do you happen to be a firefighter, a medic or a police officer or something?" She looked at me like I was crazy, so I thought that I had totally missed it. She said, "How did you know? I am a firefighter, and I am also in college to be a medic. I have been fighting lupus all my life and don't know if I will be able to fulfill my dream." She also went on to say that she was a Christian and told me that she had decided to quit her job, and this was her last day working because she felt hopeless about her future. I then prophesied over her about her future and prayed for her healing. She was visibly touched by God and thankful for the divine appointment.

You just never know who God wants to reach through your life at any given moment. This happens to me all the time and it can happen for you, but you have to continually be ready in your spirit.

"But sanctify the Lord God in your hearts, and always be ready to give a defense to everyone who asks you a reason for the hope that is in you, with meekness and fear;" 1 Peter 3:15

Right now, God is wanting to use you to reach those around you, but at the same time, the enemy is also trying to do whatever he can to take you out. The enemy does not want you to share the Gospel, give a prophetic word, pray for someone who is sick, encourage someone or give a financial blessing to someone because that will bring people closer to Jesus.

I am convinced that the reason we don't see more Christians being used by God everywhere they go is not so much out of fear (even though that is part of it), but because they are dealing with so much of their own personal issues that they have nothing left to give to others. And this is a strategy of the enemy; to keep you so focused on yourself and your problems that you have nothing left to give the world around you.

You have to start to realize the reasons why the enemy is trying to take you out. I dare you to witness or pray for someone even though you need a touch from God yourself! We need to start taking the focus off ourselves and realize that the world is bigger than the area we are currently standing in. If the enemy can keep Christians stressed out, discouraged, overwhelmed and in sin, he knows that we will not have an overflow of God in us for others. That's his plan. That's his strategy.

Here's God's strategy:

"And as you go, preach, saying, 'The Kingdom of Heaven is at hand.' Heal the sick, cleanse the lepers, raise the dead, cast out demons. Freely you have received, freely give." Matthew 10:7-8

"As you go…" Go where? As you go grocery shopping, to the mall, to get gas, to church, to your friend's house, to your neighbor's house or anywhere else, bring the Kingdom of God and share the good things that God has done for you.

My friend, it's not about preaching or working in a paid ministry position. It's simply about being a Christian with a testimony. Anyone can share what God has done. Don't let the enemy steal from you the joy of your salvation.

Beloved, you are the answer to the Lord's prayer:

"Therefore pray the Lord of the harvest to send out laborers into His harvest." Matthew 9:38

What would start to happen to this world if every Christian began to testify everywhere of how Jesus has changed their life? We would have another Great Awakening!

Now, when it comes to bringing the Kingdom of Heaven to the world around you, if the enemy can't get you to yield to the pressures of this life (to keep you quiet), he will try to assail you with persecution. He will not only have people come against what God has done for you, but he will also come against all that you stand for and all that you believe in God. He tries to weaken our foundation to see if our hearts are truly anchored in God and His Word.

"Yes, and all who desire to live godly in Christ Jesus will suffer persecution." 2 Timothy 3:12

I have had my share of being persecuted by people that I have shared Jesus with, from being knocked out cold to being spit in the face. Of course, this is absolutely nothing compared to my friends who are giving their lives for the Gospel in places around the world where you can be killed for believing in Jesus.

You see, your life—your walk with God—disrupts the forces of darkness. The enemy does not want you sharing the love and power of God to anyone. He wants you to stay in a cozy cocoon of religion where there's an, "I won't bother you, and you don't bother me" mentality.

The land that you are walking on contains the blood of the martyrs who freely gave their lives for the cause of Jesus and spreading the Gospel. It's tragically recorded in "Foxes Book of Martyrs" of the multitudes of men, women and children that went on before us and paved the way for the Christianity that we hold dear to our hearts today. And of course, men, women and children are still being persecuted and dying around the world for taking a stand for Jesus.

Wherever you are reading this book, the persecution for standing up for Jesus may or may not mean you will be killed. Either way, I can assure you that the enemy wants you quiet about what you believe. He will provoke people to yell and curse at you, reject and humiliate you, and say all kinds of evil about you.

"Blessed are you when they revile and persecute you, and say all kinds of evil against you falsely for My sake." Matthew 5:11

It's time that you decide once and for all that you are not going to let the enemy use anyone to stop you from sharing your testimony and faith in God with others.

"For I am not ashamed of the gospel of Christ, for it is the power of God to salvation for everyone who believes, for the Jew first and also for the Greek." Romans 1:16

Sure, people will mistreat you, misunderstand you, laugh at you and mock you. However, many will listen to you. They want to hear your story. They *do* want to know about Jesus. People *do* want to be loved and to know that God cares for them. Tell them with great joy and confidence that Jesus has saved you, set you free, or given you a miracle, that the Father's love is the greatest thing you have experienced in this life, and that they can experience it as well!

"He has made everything beautiful in its time. Also He has put eternity in their hearts, except that no one can find out the work that God does from beginning to end." Ecclesiastes 3:11

Unfortunately, we are not just persecuted for our testimony of God's goodness outside the four walls of the church. The enemy will also try to take you out by using people *within* the walls of the church. In other words, being rejected by a stranger because of your stand for God doesn't cut to the heart as much as when a brother or sister in church treats you poorly because of your testimony about what God has done for you.

Always remember that people criticize what they don't agree with or understand. However, you're not going to *make* anyone believe you. The enemy will find that person(s) in the church that is not yielded to the Holy Spirit or is dealing with personal issues or is in sin to try to get to you to keep you quiet. If you have been in church long enough, you have met these people. They are being used by the enemy to sow discord, pull you out of the Spirit and distract you from what God is telling you to do. That's the nicest way I can say it!

Recognize that this is a tactic of the enemy to discourage you from flowing in the Spirit and sharing what God has done for you. Stand strong, walk in love towards others and stay the course, God has a wonderful plan for you.

So, what is your testimony? What has God done for you? It's a wonderful thing to use a testimony when ministering to someone. I love this quote by C.S. Lewis:

"Friendship is born at that moment when one person says to another: '"What! You too? I thought I was the only one!"'

Take someone who is struggling in their faith out for a coffee, and share with them how God has always seen you through. Give someone who is struggling financially a blessing, and tell them, "I've been there. Here's some money to help you through this hard time." Tell the cashier who you have never met before that Jesus loves her and has a wonderful plan for her life. Put your arm around someone at church that needs to be loved because you know what it feels like to be unloved. You see how these simple moments can change a person's life? *That's* why the enemy is trying to shut you down, because you have something to say!

I want to also encourage you to get your story into a book. Write about what God has done for you and your family. Who cares if you sell only four copies? Raise some money, and give your book away everywhere you go. Your story is going to minister and encourage someone else, and you are also giving the devil a black eye every time you hand one out! Every time you open your mouth and share, write a blog (someone reading this is supposed to be blogging), post on social media, write a book, preach, teach, or send an encouraging email, you're telling the enemy, "You thought you had me. You thought I gave up. You thought you won. But I am here because of Jesus, and I am going to tell everyone your secrets and glorify God through my testimony any chance I get!" This has nothing to do with building your ministry, it's about building the Kingdom— building lives. The Lord is speaking to me that He has been telling someone who is reading this that they have been delaying writing a book, and the Lord says, "It's time, do it."

"If we suffer persecution and affliction in a right manner, we attain a larger measure of conformity to Christ, by a due improvement of one of these occasions, than we could have done merely by imitating His mercy, in abundance of good works" John Wesley

6

HIDDEN PLACES OF THE HEART

"Prayer does not mean simply to pour out one's heart. It means rather to find the way to God and speak with Him, whether the heart is full or empty" Dietrich Bonhoeffer; German pastor, theologian, prisoner, hanged by the Nazi's

You know, Jesus specializes in healing the broken-hearted. No matter what the enemy tries to do to your heart, Jesus can heal it. Jesus forgives and heals everything.

"Who forgives all your iniquities, who heals all your diseases," Psalm 103:3

Another way that the enemy is trying to take you out is by exposing and exploiting what is lying dormant within your heart. Anything within your heart that has not been dealt with through repentance, healing, renewing, forgiveness or deliverance, the enemy will try to use against you.

Right now, your soul is carrying (in those areas that have not been dealt with) the sum of everything that you've been through in life, all that's happened to you, all that people have done or said to you, everything that's hurt or wounded you or has brought you shame. That may seem overwhelming to you right now, but the Lord wants you to deal with those things, so the enemy no longer has a foothold in your life.

It's obviously no secret that each one of us goes through so much in this life. Some of it is our own fault, and some of it is not. Some things that we have been through have been easier to deal with than other things. For instance, my Father died of cancer when I was twelve, and that affected me deeply. Then when I was 18, I was in a high speed head-on collision in which God spared the lives of those in our car as well as any serious or lasting pain and trauma.

Those are *just two* of the many things that have happened to me, and I'm sure that many of you have experienced similar things and much, much worse. The idea here is not to compare one person's life events to another, but for you to realize that we all go through pain and suffering, and the pain and suffering that you have been through affected you in one way or another. We should never compare what we go through with others, because everyone deals with things differently. Something that you have been through may not affect me like it affected you and vice versa. The key is to have compassion with everyone, no matter how big or small you feel their problem is. You truly don't know how it's affecting their heart.

"Blessed be the God and Father of our Lord Jesus Christ, the Father of mercies and God of all comfort, who comforts us in all our tribulation, that we may be able to comfort those who are in any trouble, with the comfort with which we ourselves are comforted by God." 2 Corinthians 1:3-4

Jesus paid a dear price so that you can live free, inside and out. His blood is enough to cover anything that you have been through. The enemy wants to take you out by making you feel that you will never be healed or free from what has happened to you—those hidden places of your heart. Until those hidden places are completely given over to Jesus, the enemy will use those things against you. It could be trauma that you have been through, secret sin, unforgiveness, generational curses, etc. Typically, undealt with areas are the origin of open doors for the enemy to come and bring shame, depression, fear, hopelessness, financial lack, grief, sickness, and the list goes on and on. Do you see how important it is to take care of these things within your heart? Aren't you tired of dealing with the same issues over and over again? Aren't you fed up with the rollercoaster of emotions you deal with because of heart issues? It's time to break these ungodly cycles you have been facing. My heart completely goes out to you—been there, done that. More on that later.

I want to ask you a question: What is it that's bothering you? What is upsetting you? Where are you hurt? Where are you broken? What lies have you believed about yourself? Where is there unforgiveness? In what ways are you blaming God for things that have happened? Are you battling shame? Maybe fear? Are you not feeling loved? Where is there still a "sting" in your heart because of what has happened to you? What areas in your life are you overlooking in your own heart and blaming others for your pain, stress, grief and problems? Beloved, it's your choice if you're going to keep hanging on to what you're hanging on to. What is the Holy Spirit revealing to you about your heart even while you are reading this? In the space provided below, please feel free to write down those areas in your life that you feel the Holy Spirit is highlighting to bring healing to your heart.

THE HOLY SPIRIT IS SHOWING ME:

_____

_____

_____

_____

_____

_____

_____

_____

_____

_____

_____

_____

_____

_____

_____

_____

_____

_____

_____

_____

_____

_____

_____

_____

_____

_____

_____

We sometimes unwittingly create an unhealthy unity within our hearts with those negative things that we have been through. It's called living in protection mode. It's walls that we have built up around our hearts to protect us from any more hurt, shame or rejection. The problem with these walls is that it also keeps us from experiencing Father's best for us. Father wants us to prosper in our souls and not become hardened to Him or others.

"Beloved, I pray that you may prosper in all things and be in health, just as your soul prospers." 3 John 1:2

Today, why don't you surrender those hidden areas in your heart to God, once and for all? Any area that we have in our heart that is not healed is an opportunity for an evil spirit to find entrance into our lives to mess with us, get us addicted, bring shame, bring depression, make us physically sick, etc. Sometimes long-term sickness, disease and pain can be tied in with a wounded soul. So, don't be surprised if you also get physically healed as your heart becomes healed!

RECEIVING FATHER'S LOVE

You have a story and a history; we all do. Just one of the things I have been through in life was losing my dad to cancer when I was 12 years old. Prior to his death, he had been sick for five years, so I really didn't get to know my dad at all. He was a Christian, so I will see him again one day, but that was little comfort to a young boy who had just lost his dad. Again, I am not comparing my story to anyone else, because we all respond differently to issues. I am simply telling you what happened to me. I loved my dad even though I only have a few vague memories (it's been over 35 years since he has been gone).

After my dad's death, I went from being a straight A student to getting F's in many of my classes. I was broken, wounded, hurt, grieved and angry. My young heart felt abandoned and rejected. I didn't feel the love of God, and I had a lot of questions like, "How come God couldn't stop my dad from dying?" My family loved the Lord very much, and we always put Him first in our family. I held on to these things in my heart for a number of years, and because I was so wounded, this inner turmoil led to depression, sin, shame, rejection, etc. I needed to be healed. I needed to experience the love of Father God for myself. So, I went on my own journey to find the Father's love...

Here's what I did (and this can work for any area of your life, trust me): I began to listen to anyone I could find that taught on experiencing the Father's love. My favorite teachers on the Father heart of God are Mike Bickle, John and Carol Arnott and Jack Frost. I would listen to their teachings over and over again. I would study and study what they taught. For how long? Until it became part of me. The journey went from reading/listening to their teaching to it becoming a revelation, then I would apply it to my life until it became part of me. This was not an overnight experience. I paid the price to get my heart healed and replace the wounds with the truth of the Father's heart for me.

I then did my own studies on the life of David, the Psalms and the Song of Solomon until that became part of my DNA as well. I took scriptures and studied them over and over again. Then I would take those same verses and pray and meditate on them. Then I started to really, really believe what I was reading in the Word of God! It became part of me from the inside out. I owned it for myself to the point that—now hear this carefully—to the point that I never even hear a whisper from the enemy about anything contrary to Father's love for me. Why is that? There is no reason for the enemy to trouble me in the area of the Father's love because it's pointless on his end. Does that mean that I am someone special? To Father God, yes! We all are! But I am nothing special in the natural. I simply chose to run after the heart of God and take care of my own heart, and now I teach others on how to experience the love of the Father for themselves.

When you live loved, it's difficult for the enemy to get to you, because he knows that you know how much Father God loves you and is looking out for you. It's about knowing, believing and receiving. You can't just know about His love. You have to believe that He loves YOU and then receive and walk in His love every day.

Many Christians today still struggle with Father's love for them. They know that God loves them, but receiving that love and living loved is a different story. Here's a very simple analogy that will help you: Let's say that my son is standing next to me, and then someone gives him a bunch of books to hold on to. Then someone else gives him some groceries to carry. Then someone else puts on his back a heavy backpack. On top of all of this, someone hands him some bricks to also carry. Do you get the visual? Here's my son holding all this stuff that he's doing his best to carry and balance. Let's say all that "stuff" represented all those things that we go through in life such as marriage issues, financial issues, pain in our body, relationship problems, you name it. We hold on to and carry more than we realize (again refer to the list that you wrote earlier in this book), and we don't realize how much it's affecting our lives and walk with Father God. Ok, now, let's say while my son is holding on to all of that "stuff", he asks for me to give him a hug. It would be difficult to wrap my arms around my son and all the stuff that he's carrying at the same time. I am able to do it, but it just doesn't feel the same to him. I am telling him I love him. I can see that he's struggling with all of that stuff he's holding on to, but it's difficult for him to feel the embrace of my hug because of all that he's carrying.

Are the Father's arms big and powerful enough to embrace us even though we are holding on to so much? Of course! But we don't *feel* His touch like we should because of what we are holding, and it has nothing to do with the Father's nearness to us. Are you starting to get it? It's difficult to feel the wonderful embrace of the Father's love when we are also embracing unforgiveness, pain, rejection, shame, etc., at the same time.

Here's what I would tell my son to do in the natural: "Let me take all that stuff you are holding on to. I can handle it, I'm your strong Father." And as he gives me all those things he was holding, he will literally feel the weights lifting off of him. Then when he says, "Dad, will you give me another hug?", there is nothing in the way, and my son can fully experience my arms around him as I embrace him with my love.

Beloved, it's never about Father God's ability to love you through even your darkest times. His love for you is far greater than you can even imagine. Right now, He loves you with the full extent of His love. It's about letting go of those things that you are carrying so that you can experience the love He's ALREADY giving you! Friends, when you live loved from the inside out, it changes the way you live in every other area of your life.

"Behold what manner of love the Father has bestowed on us, that we should be called children of God!" 1 John 3:1

"But You, O Lord, are a God full of compassion, and gracious, longsuffering and abundant in mercy and truth." Psalm 86:15

"And we have known and believed the love that God has for us. God is love, and he who abides in love abides in God, and God in him." 1 John 4:16

Just like me, you have your own story, and the truth is, it doesn't have to take years and years before you feel healed and whole. In His presence, anything can happen at any moment. You are already changing after reading this, I can feel it.

A HEALED MARRIAGE

I watched a video on YouTube about a story that came out of the Toronto Blessing which was a powerful move of God led by John and Carol Arnott that had its peak in the 1990's. The video was of a couple being interviewed because they had received such a powerful touch from God. During the interview, this couple could hardly talk because they were laughing so hard. They were actually laughing so hard that they were crying and could hardly stand up! The interviewer was asking them what happened, what's going on? Referring to her husband, the wife said, "I hated him (as she was laughing!). Our marriage was doomed; it was a bad marriage. I wanted to kill him; I wanted to burn all his stuff!

I would chase him around the house with knives!" She went on to say that the marriage counselor they had been going to even said there was no hope or help for them. As they were totally, "drunk in the Spirit", the interviewer asked again what happened, and she talked about how there was now so much love and happiness in her heart. She said that Jesus completely changed her life from the inside out, and she just loves everybody! Friends, only Jesus can do that! Only Jesus can heal the broken hearted. At the end of the interview, while she was laughing, she pointed to her husband and said, "This is my big love!" The enemy has no chance against a marriage that is healed, whole and full of joy and love!

SIGNS OF A HEALED HEART

Beloved, I don't want the enemy to exploit any hidden areas within your heart to keep you spinning in circles for the rest of your life. You see, when you're healed and whole, you feel different, you look different, you act different, you talk different, you live loved all the time and express that love to the world around you. It's truly a wonderful way to live each and every day.

Friend, I don't care who you are, one of the things that you crave the most in life is to be loved, adored and enjoyed. Whether you are a CEO of a major company, a pastor of a church, a warehouse worker or a celebrity, you desire to be loved whether you express that desire to others or not.

Remember, God *is* love. That's not just His personality. He is love, and He put the desire to love and be loved into all of us.

Here are several signs of a person with a heart that has been healed and is walking in wholeness:

WHAT ARE YOU TALKING ABOUT?

A healed heart shares about the pain of the past only to minister to someone else who is going through similar circumstances or as a testimony bringing glory to God. You've been around those individuals, I'm sure, that can hardly go through a meaningful conversation without their troubled past being unconsciously revealed yet again. You have to understand that whatever you have been through, the "historical memory" won't change. Good, bad or ugly, it happened somewhere in your past. However, the good news is that the horrible "sting" that the memory left behind can be removed by the healing power of God to the point that you don't feel the hurt, pain, trauma and shame of those events any longer.

"Blessed be the God and Father of our Lord Jesus Christ, the Father of mercies and God of all comfort, who comforts us in all our tribulation, that we may be able to comfort those who are in any trouble, with the comfort with which we ourselves are comforted by God." II Corinthians 1:3-4

DON'T OVERREACT

A healed heart does not react to people that try to hurt you, rather it responds to them in love. When there is an unhealed area in our lives, we tend to overreact when others try to hurt us. The enemy is good at using others to try to get wounded hearts to completely overreact in even the most minor of circumstances.

"But I tell you not to resist an evil person. But whoever slaps you on your right cheek, turn the other to him also...love your enemies, bless those who curse you, do good to those who hate you, and pray for those who spitefully use you and persecute you..." Matthew 5:39, 44

A CARRIER OF PEACE

A healed heart has a real peace about life. Your heart is not full of turmoil, unrest, anxiety and stress, which the enemy tries to do his best to inflict upon us. A healed heart walks in the true peace of God, because the God-kind of peace comes from within.

"You will keep him in perfect peace, whose mind is stayed on You, because he trusts in You." Isaiah 26:3

"Be anxious for nothing, but in everything by prayer and supplication, with thanksgiving, let your requests be made known to God; and the peace of God, which surpasses all understanding, will guard your hearts and minds through Christ Jesus." Philippians 4:6-7

A JOYFUL HEART

A healed heart has a joy that can literally been seen in the eyes, no matter what someone has been through. The pain that you have been through has been replaced by the indescribable joy of the Lord from deep within. And as with peace, true joy is birthed from the inside out.

"You will show me the path of life; In Your presence is fullness of joy; At Your right hand are pleasures forevermore." Psalm 16:11

"...Do not sorrow, for the joy of the LORD is your strength."
Nehemiah 8:10

TALK OF HIS GOODNESS

A healed heart loves to talk about the goodness and love of the Father, because the things of this world pale in comparison. A heart that has found its anchor in the Father's love can't help but share with others how wonderful He is. You can hear it when they talk; there is a real sweetness in their tone as you can feel the presence of Jesus when they talk to you. The truth is, they have spent much time sitting at the feet of Jesus, realizing that He is the greatest in all the world.

"Let no corrupt word proceed out of your mouth, but what is good for necessary edification, that it may impart grace to the hearers." Ephesians 4:29

"Let the word of Christ dwell in you richly in all wisdom, teaching and admonishing one another in psalms and hymns and spiritual songs, singing with grace in your hearts to the Lord." Colossians 3:16

DON'T HOLD ON TO "STUFF"

A healed heart does not hold on to bitterness, offense and unforgiveness. These are some of the enemy's favorite strongholds. As a Christian, if you struggle in any of these areas, that is a true sign of an area in your heart that has not been dealt with.

We all have many opportunities to take offense with people, whether they are in the world or in church. I have watched people leave the church for the silliest reasons. As a pastor, I have been blindsided by those who took offense at something I said or did, and they held it against me. All the while, I was clueless that they felt the way they did. What they never seemed to realize is how much I truly loved them. Paul said it this way in *2 Corinthians 12:15, "And I will very gladly spend and be spent for your souls; though the more abundantly I love you, the less I am loved."* Ministers have to be very careful to not get into offense, bitterness and unforgiveness because that can do damage to the ministry, as well as your own heart.

Are there areas in your life that you are holding on to offense, bitterness or unforgiveness? You must give those things over to God. Did someone hurt you, mistreat you or misunderstand you, causing you to be wounded? I'm sure they did. The only way to heal is to love and forgive the way Jesus has loved and forgiven you and I for everything we have done. Sometimes you can go to the person that hurt you and in love, make things right. Either way, if you are going to hold on to your wound, the responsibility is yours and not the other person's.

"The discretion of a man makes him slow to anger, and his glory is to overlook a transgression." Proverbs 19:11

"Also do not take to heart everything people say, lest you hear your servant cursing you. For many times, also, your own heart has known that even you have cursed others." Ecclesiastes 7:21-22

"And above all things have fervent love for one another, for '"love will cover a multitude of sins."'" 1 Peter 4:8

ADDICTED TO JESUS

A healed heart is not addicted to anything except Jesus. There is no need to be comforted by counterfeit affections. The enemy wants you addicted to whatever he can get you to yield your body to. Beloved, you don't need a glass of wine "to get your peace back", you need the Holy Spirit. That last statement is not about if I think drinking wine is wrong or not. What *I am saying* is that you don't need the things of the world to receive true love, peace, joy and acceptance.

For instance, you don't need to get lost in watching tv show after tv show to hide from the reality of a broken marriage; you need healing. Another addiction is pornography, which is a sin, but it is rooted in deeper issues in the heart that need healing and deliverance. Search your heart to see if there is anything in your life that you "can't let go of" for the Lord. Let Jesus be your addiction. What does that mean? Long for Him morning, noon, night and midnight snack! Desire Him more than anything this world has to offer. Let's deal with those things in our hearts that draw us away from Him.

"O God, You are my God; Early will I seek You; My soul thirsts for You; My flesh longs for You in a dry and thirsty land where there is no water." Psalm 63:1

"One thing I have desired of the LORD, that will I seek: That I may dwell in the house of the LORD all the days of my life, to behold the beauty of the LORD, and to inquire in His temple." Psalm 27:4

A LOVING FATHER

A healed heart sees and feels God as a loving Father. A heart that is healed lives accepted and enjoyed by God. It's a heart that lives feeling like you are Father's favorite son or daughter. My son is a baseball player, and if you were to take him aside and ask him what Dad has taught him about when he steps up to the plate, he will tell you, "I've already won!" I have taught my son and daughter through the years that no matter what happens in life, no matter how successful they are, no matter what they face in life, they have already won because they have won God's heart and Dad and Mom's hearts. My kids grew up knowing that no matter what, they are loved by God and Dad and Mom.

This has anchored their hearts in the Father's love. They have heard Dad teach on the Father's love over and over again, and though I am far from perfect, they know that they are deeply loved. Remember that I already taught you that it's about removing the hinderances so that you can experience the Father's love, adoration and enjoyment over you. The enemy is clueless on what to do with a Christian that lives loved!

"For I am persuaded that neither death nor life, nor angels nor principalities nor powers, nor things present nor things to come, nor height nor depth, nor any other created thing, shall be able to separate us from the love of God which is in Christ Jesus our Lord." Romans 8:38-39

"that Christ may dwell in your hearts through faith; that you, being rooted and grounded in love, may be able to comprehend with all the saints what is the width and length and depth and height—to know the love of Christ which

passes knowledge; that you may be filled with all the fullness of God." Ephesians 3:17-19

"Now hope does not disappoint, because the love of God has been poured out in our hearts by the Holy Spirit who was given to us." Romans 5:5

"keep yourselves in the love of God..." Jude 21

A HUMBLE SPIRIT

A healed heart has a humble spirit. Much of the time, pride is the result of a root of rejection in someone's life. Instead of receiving healing, the person overcompensates for the lack that they feel within, and it manifests in the form of pride. There is a big difference between being sure of yourself and confident of who you are in Christ and walking in pride.

It is very dangerous territory when the enemy can get you to yield to having a prideful spirit. The Bible literally says that God hates pride (see Proverbs 6:16-17). Nobody can tell you anything when you have pride. You feel as if you have all the answers for everyone, all the time. You walk around as if you can do no wrong. You see how dangerous it is? Pride keeps us from experiencing the fullness of what God has for us.

"Pride goes before destruction, and a haughty spirit before a fall." Proverbs 16:18

Insecurity, low self-worth, low self-esteem and rejection need to be healed within our hearts so we can flow in the Spirit and be used by God without pride overtaking us. We need servant hearts—hearts that are filled with love and gratitude and are confident in the Father's heart for us, not hearts that have to always be recognized, be in the forefront, or have a "Look at me, notice me!" attitude.

We need to finally realize that:

"A man's gift makes room for him, and brings him before great men." Proverbs 18:16

Then we will quit striving to see who will notice us, invite us to minister, promote us, endorse us, etc. When we walk in humility, God will ALWAYS make sure that the gifts that He put within us will place us in front of the right people at the right time whether that means ministry or employment elsewhere. Strive to be a doorkeeper in the house of God, not the one who has to be in front.

"For a day in Your courts is better than a thousand. I would rather be a doorkeeper in the house of my God than dwell in the tents of wickedness." Psalm 84:10

Has the enemy been trying to take you out with pride? Repent of any pride in your life, and deal with whatever root is attached. A big part of healing is replacing the root issue with the revelation of the love of the Father and receiving His love in the areas where there had been low self-worth, rejection and insecurity.

MERCIFUL

A healed heart is merciful, compassionate and quick to forgive, knowing how much mercy, compassion and forgiveness that God has had towards you. A heart that is healed is not hard-hearted towards others. From CEO's to the homeless, you long to show mercy and compassion to others because of all that Jesus has done for you. A healed heart is quick to forgive your brothers and sisters, because you know that God has does the same for you.

"With the merciful You will show Yourself merciful..." 2 Samuel 22:26

"Therefore, as the elect of God, holy and beloved, put on tender mercies, kindness, humility, meekness, longsuffering; bearing with one another, and forgiving on another, if anyone has a complaint against another; even as Christ forgave you, so you also must do." Colossians 3:12-13

HONOR AUTHORITY

A healed heart honors those that God has placed in authority in your life. You no longer see pastors, leaders and those in authority as a threat or a source of pain because of past bad experiences. If you have been in church long enough, you have seen leaders who use their position to manipulate and control others. This does not mean that all leadership is bad. The enemy wants to put something in your heart towards leaders so you don't ever find stability in ministry, especially in the local church. God has put men and women in authority in our lives to help us and equip us to fulfill all that God has for our lives.

"And He Himself gave some to be apostles, some prophets, some evangelists, and some pastors and teachers, for the equipping of the saints for the work o ministry, for the edifying of the body of Christ, till we all come to the unity of the faith and of the knowledge of the Son of God, to a perfect man, to the measure of the stature of the fullness of Christ;" Ephesians 4:11-13

NO SHAME

A healed heart does not live with a spirit of shame and condemnation. A heart that is healed lives forgiven and accepted because of the blood of Jesus. Sometimes it's hard to believe we are forgiven, because we don't always *feel* forgiven. But we have to take God at His Word:

"Bless the LORD, O my soul; and all that is within me, bless His holy name! Bless the LORD, O my soul, and forget not all His benefits: Who forgives all your iniquities, who heals all your diseases, who redeems your life from destruction, who crowns you with lovingkindness and tender mercies...

The LORD is merciful and gracious, slow to anger, and abounding in mercy. He will not always strive with us, nor will He keep His anger forever. He has not dealt with us according to our sins, nor punished us according to our iniquities. For as the heavens are high above the earth, so great is His mercy toward those who fear Him; As far as the east is from the west, so far has He removed our transgressions from us. As a father pities his children, so the LORD pities those who fear Him." Psalm 103:1-4, 8-13

No matter what you have done, if you have asked Jesus to forgive you, it has been washed in His blood. You have no past in the Lord's eyes. You must grab ahold of that truth by faith. Shame and condemnation are two favorites of the enemy to keep you in a small place. There are many Christians that struggle with shame and condemnation, and it leads to discouragement, disappointment in self, depression and more sin which, in turn, leads to more shame.

I meet believers everywhere affected by shame. They have trouble holding their head up when they are around people; they feel like a fake; they feel like everyone looks down on them (whether others know their past or not); and they feel like they can't forgive themselves. All these emotions are the enemy's plan to keep you from moving forward in God. If shame has its way in our lives, it will stunt our growth in God. Again, we have to believe that God's Word is the truth, not what we feel on the inside:

"If we confess our sins, He is faithful and just to forgive us our sins and to cleanse us from all unrighteousness." 1 John 1:9

When we do our part, God does His part. What is it in your past that you are still feeling shame and condemnation about? How has it been affecting your life? They enemy may have been trying to take you out for something God already forgave you for a long time ago. You may have to forgive yourself. Beloved, trust in the blood of Jesus. Trust in His love and power to forgive you of all your sins. Yes, that thing happened in your life, and you can't take it back. You may have a "historical record" of something that you did wrong or even a lifetime of bad choices, but just know that God is bigger than any sin(s) you have committed and has erased the sinful history of all those that have repented. He's a good Father, and He loves you with all His heart.

"I, even I, am He who blots out your transgressions for My own sake; And I will not remember your sins." Isaiah 43:25

"Come now, and let us reason together,"' Says the LORD, '"Though your sins and like scarlet, they shall be as white as

snow; though they are red like crimson, they shall be as wool"' Isaiah 1:18

"Therefore, if anyone is in Christ, he is a new creation; old things have passed away; behold, all things have become new." 2 Corinthians 5:17

QUICK TO REPENT

Finally, a healed heart is quick to repent. A heart that is healed does not hold on to anything that can hinder or damage your relationship with the Lord. When you sin, you are quick to seek forgiveness from God and others. I have had well known ministers tell me personally that they live a lifestyle of repentance. I like that. It's not a sin-consciousness mentality—far from it. Rather, it's a life that walks in the fear of the Lord and knows that holiness is very pleasing to God. It's a heart with no secret or hidden sin attached to it.

"Or do you despise the riches of His goodness, forbearance, and longsuffering, not knowing that the goodness of God leads you to repentance?" Romans 2:4

"Purge me with hyssop, and I shall be clean; Wash me, and I shall be whiter than snow." Psalm 51:7

The reason why many Christians go through their entire lives with their hearts unhealed is because the power of their souls (mind, will and emotions) is too strong. As a pastor, working with people, I have struggled and struggled with this principle. It seems like no matter how much you teach, pray, prophesy, love, serve and give to people, some refuse to change. Why is that? I believe that they feel that the issues within their heart seem greater than the reality of God's power to break their strongholds and bring them to a place of wholeness and healing.

As pastors, we have exhausted all of our efforts on entire families that choose to stay in a small place and not take care of heart issues. We love them dearly, but they make their own choices to stay broken on the inside. The enemy can have a field day with a heart that chooses to hold on to all those things we described in this chapter.

If your heart is unhealed in any of the areas that I mentioned (or those I didn't mention, of course), you can be healed and free today! Follow these simple principles below to bring lasting healing to your heart:

1. Recognize your need for change.
2. Repent of all sins associated with an orphan spirit.
3. Forgive others and yourself, as this will bring a supernatural release in your heart.
4. Refuse to return to any ungodly beliefs that you once carried within your heart. Here are some examples of ungodly beliefs: Nobody loves me, no one appreciates me, I am not pretty or handsome, I'll never be married, I will always struggle, I always embarrass myself, I'm never going to have enough money, I never feel God's love, etc. What ungodly beliefs are you still battling with? You may need to refer to what you wrote down earlier. Whatever those things are, ask the Lord to forgive you, and then replace the ungodly beliefs with the truth from God's Word in that area. At the end of this book, I give you many Scriptures that have been

personalized that you can use to help you know who you are in Christ.

5. Keep yourselves in the love of the Father every day. Stay close to the Lord each day by meditating on the Word, staying in continual prayer, worshipping Him often and praying in your heavenly language as much as possible. This will keep your spirit strong and cause you to grow and mature in the things of God.

Now remember, anything in your life left undealt with will be something the enemy will try to use against you. That's why everything is about to change for the better for you; I really believe that! It's a new day!

"Through the LORD'S mercies we are not consumed, because His compassions fail not. They are new every morning; great is Your faithfulness." Lamentations 3:22-23

In these verses in Lamentations, it is made abundantly clear that God loves and believes in you! He knew exactly what he was getting into when He created and called you. He did not make a mistake. You are not a mistake. You are not a hopeless hypocrite. You are His Beloved!

I want to end this chapter by paraphrasing these two verses from Lamentations for you as I have studied them out for myself:

"Because of the Lord's incredible favor and covenant loyalty that He has towards you, you are not finished. This is not your end but only the beginning! Father God will never cease

to pour out His love to you, as His love comes from the deepest place within His heart—a love so deep, intimate and tender that it will heal the deepest longing within you. This morning, Father loves you with the SAME refreshing love and mercy that He had for you yesterday when you felt like you failed Him in a particular area. Father's love and faithfulness is in great abundance for you—there's more than enough for everyone to receive it every day"
Lamentations 3:22-23, my paraphrase

KILLING LAZARUS

7

BEYOND BREAKTHROUGH

"It's rigged in your favor; How would you live if you knew you wouldn't fail?" Dr. Kevin Zadai

Ok, you got this far in the book. Now you know why and how the enemy has been trying to take you out. This entire chapter is dedicated to helping you move beyond breakthrough. What do I mean? Aren't you tired of just going from conference to conference, meeting to meeting, book to book, Bible study to Bible study just to get another breakthrough to keep you going for another day, week or month? We have to learn the art of digging our heels in and not letting the enemy have any more say so in our lives. I have already exposed to you the strategies of the enemy to take you out in this life. Now it's up to you to apply those principles, move beyond breakthrough and live in the continuous supply of the Lord's blessing and favor in every area of your life—every day.

"They are abundantly satisfied with the fullness of Your

house, and You give them drink from the river of Your pleasures." Psalm 36:8

DON'T LOSE HEART

As a pastor, I have made the mistake of trying to win people's battles in the spirit for them. I can't win your victories for you; you have to go get yourself your own victories. I am here to help; that's why I wrote this book, but I can't *make you do anything*. I can't make you pray. I can't make you fight. I can't make you believe and trust God. I can't make you worship. I can't make you be a witness for God. I can't make you beat up the devil. You have to do all those things yourself if you are going to see major changes in your life and move beyond breakthrough.

I want you to get to the place in God where you are continually enjoying His presence and are not caught up in the drama of this world. I want to help you break out of the cycle of simply going from one breakthrough to the next and start living out of your spirit every day. One of the greatest keys is found in 2 Corinthians:

"Therefore we do not lose heart. Even though our outward man is perishing, yet the inward man is being renewed day by day. For our light affliction, which is but for a moment, is working for us a far more exceeding and eternal weight of glory, while we do not look at the things which are seen, but at the things which are not seen. For the things which are seen are temporary, but the things which are not seen are

eternal." II Corinthians 4:16-18

Beloved, you can't lose your heart. Paul is encouraging us to stay in there with God and not get fainthearted or overwhelmed. Yes, our outward man is perishing; we are getting older, not younger. However, we take great joy in knowing that our inward man is being renewed, strengthened and invigorated every day! Every day we have the opportunity to sit at His feet, be filled with His presence and be strengthened in our spirit. We don't have to wrap up this life on earth being beat up, worn out and discouraged on the inside. We can finish strong and full of joy on the inside, no matter what our body looks or feels like on the outside.

The key is having eternal eyes that are fixed on the glory that awaits us, rather than the momentary afflictions currently around us. Everything you see around you is temporary. Whatever you're going through, no matter how dire—it's temporary. And I prophesy that deliverance is coming to you!

"Many are the afflictions of the righteous, but the LORD delivers him out of them all." Psalm 34:19

That's a promise! You are going to be delivered out of everything you are going through. There is an end in sight. Ask God to give you eyes to see the eternal. The enemy wants you to only look at what's around you; the pain, the suffering, the bills, the lack, etc. To have God's perspective and to see with eternal eyes is to understand that God has your future already mapped out for you, and it's good!

"For I know the thoughts that I think toward you, says the LORD, thoughts of peace and not of evil, to give you a future and a hope. Then you will call upon Me and go and pray to Me, and I will listen to you. And you will seek Me and find Me, when you search for Me with all your heart." Jeremiah 29:11-13

They key is that we must fight the temptation to "coast" in our walk with God and guard our hearts from becoming dull and careless, but rather daily renew our hearts in the fire of His love. Again, our outward man may be perishing, but our inward man is an entirely different story. As I have taught you, the enemy is after what is on the inside, because that's what really matters. If you can keep the fire burning hot within you, if you can keep your joy, if you can keep your peace, if you can keep your love strong, every day, nothing the enemy throws at you will stand in your way for long. Something has to give in, and it might as well be the devil.

A BEAUTIFUL MESS

I understand that sometimes things in life don't always go the way we hoped they would. Things may look or feel "messy" in your life right now, but I want to share with you that no matter what things look like on the outside, you're beautiful on the inside. Man or woman, you are beautiful to Father God.

They say that beauty is in the eye of the beholder and you are the one that Father is beholding—that makes you beautiful no matter what mess you are finding yourself in right now. When we receive His priceless love into our hearts, we can walk in the confidence that we are the one who God loves.

The young woman in Song of Solomon 1:5 expressed it like this:

"I am dark but lovely…"

She is saying, "No matter what has happened around me or what I have been through, please don't define me by what I look like outwardly, because I am lovely on the inside. My heart is lovely to Jesus no matter what you think."

And then King David said it this way:

"But I am poor and needy; yet the LORD thinks upon me…"
Psalm 40:17

King David knew the reality of his own life and heart, but despite everything, he knew that Father God was thinking about him. Those thoughts are beautifully expressed in many of the Psalms.

So, you may feel like a mess. Your life may feel like a mess. Your past may feel like a mess. Your finances may feel like a mess. Your marriage may feel like a mess. But despite all the mess, you are beautiful to Father God. His love and heart for you transcend the mess that you are in. To go beyond breakthrough despite all the mess around you, this is where you have to start: by reminding yourself that Father loves you and is in your corner cheering you on.

Today, begin to lift yourself out of the mess by first realizing that through it all, you are beautiful before God. You belong to Father God, and He loves you with all His heart, but you have to believe it and receive it. Receiving His love for you will restore and strengthen your heart as you move forward in victory.

Now, take each "mess", lift it up before God and say:

"I am deeply loved, so God, you got this. Show me what to do. I repent for living in my mess and not from a heart that is loved. I want to move beyond breakthrough. Forgive me for yielding to those things that don't please your heart. Lead and guide me out of the messes that I am in, and bring me to a place of victory and joy in every area of my life. Amen"

ARMED AND DANGEROUS

As I said earlier, I have the opportunity to work with the police department. I have seen many law-breakers handcuffed, placed in the back of police cars and sent to jail. And I have learned that catching these criminals in the natural is much like catching devils in the spirit realm!

Have you ever had a police car pull up behind you and you

start getting nervous, even though your vehicle is completely legal and you have done nothing wrong? Why do we feel that way? Because we know the authority that the badge carries. And if you have done something wrong, that officer has the authority to write you a ticket or put handcuffs on you and even take you to jail. Again, the officer has this right because they are walking in their authority. It doesn't mean that every criminal is going to be peacefully handcuffed. Sometimes it takes more than one officer to help with a situation, and the criminal is arrested and put in jail.

As Christians, because of the name and blood of Jesus, we have supernatural authority to "handcuff" the devil and lock him away, never to trouble us again. And just like the police officers, sometimes we have to call in for a little back up—a little extra prayer support, because not all devils leave easily.

I am sharing this analogy with you because you have been troubled and tormented by devils long enough. It's time to move beyond breakthrough and into ongoing freedom and victory.

"And Jesus came and spoke to them, saying, '"All authority has been given to Me in heaven and on earth. Go therefore and make disciples of all the nations, baptizing them in the name of the Father and of the Son and of the Holy Spirit, teaching them to observe all things I have commanded you:

and lo, I am with you always, even to the end of the age.'"
Matthew 28:18-20

Beloved, all authority has been given to Jesus. He is the name above all names (see Philippians 2:9-11), and it's His name that we use to drive out demons:

"And these signs will follow those who believe: In My name they will cast out demons; they will speak with new tongues; they will take up serpents; and if they drink anything deadly, it will by no means hurt them; they will lay hands on the sick, and they will recover." Mark 16:17-18

Demon spirits have limited power, and let me tell you, they are good at masking their limitations. They want you to feel as if you will never get free, that you will never get a breakthrough and that you will always be bound. The enemy tries to hide his limitations by making God's children feel overwhelmed, burned out, and discouraged and as if the situation you are in is impossible to overcome.

Don't ever forget this: the enemy's power is so limited that he has to tempt you to give in! He can't *make* you give in or give up, but he can certainly tempt you to do so. The enemy is like the proverbial junkyard dog. He looks fierce, barking strong and loud, showing his teeth, foaming at the mouth and acting like he wants to eat you for lunch. The closer you get to the junkyard dog, the more ferocious it seems. And then it starts coming after you when all of a sudden, the dog is yanked back by its chain, because it will allow him to only go so far, and it never reached you. The junkyard dog has limitations. The enemy coming after you has limitations. When you turn to the enemy and say, "You have come close enough! In the name of Jesus, leave me and my family alone, now!" according to the promises of the Word of God, the enemy has to go.

When you understand how truly armed and dangerous you really are to the kingdom of darkness, everything around you begins to change. You become a person that quits putting up with the devil's tactics. This is when you have moved beyond breakthrough.

Right now would be a good time for you to repent for any areas that you have allowed the enemy to have his way with you and your family (whatever the Holy Spirit brings to mind). Break any legal right the enemy has had to mess with you. Drive the enemy out by the name and blood of Jesus and declare that he no longer has a place in your home. Show the enemy that you mean business and that you are not going to tolerate him anymore.

When the enemy perceives that you mean business, desiring to live pure and not putting up with him any longer, he may try to attack you another way, but whatever you do, do not give up. Remember, YOU are the one with the power and authority that is greater than any evil force trying to come against you. Keep pushing back every time the enemy tries to push you. When the enemy comes against you one way, make him pay and flee from you seven ways (see

Deuteronomy 28:7). Just don't ever give up, no matter how dire the circumstances may seem. It's time to move beyond breakthrough and into continuous victory!

YOU'RE NOT LOST

As we go through life, we can sometimes feel like we are getting lost in the midst of all that is happening around us. Life itself can really take its toll on hearts that are not firmly rooted in Father's love. To move beyond breakthrough, you will need to learn to trust and obey God unconditionally. If you yield your heart to him, He will faithfully guide you through any storm and circumstance.

"Trust in the LORD with all your heart, and lean not on your own understanding; In all your ways acknowledge Him, and He shall direct your paths." Proverbs 3:5-6

He is the one that is to be ordering our steps and directing our paths.

"The steps of a good man are ordered by the LORD, and He delights in his way." Psalm 37:23

Why do you think Jesus was asleep in the boat while at the same time the disciples were freaking out?

"Now when He got into a boat, His disciples followed Him. And suddenly a great tempest arose on the sea, so that the boat was covered with the waves. But He was asleep. Then

His disciples came to Him and awoke Him, saying, '"Lord, save us! We are perishing!"' But He said to them, '"Why are you fearful, O you of little faith?"' Then He arose and rebuked the winds and the sea, and there was a great calm. So the men marveled, saying, '"Who can this be, that even the winds and the sea obey Him?"' When He had come to the other side, to the country of the Gergesenes, there met Him two demon-possessed men, coming out of the tombs, exceedingly fierce, so that no one could pass that way." Matthew 8:23-28

Jesus was asleep because He already knew from His Father that there was a job to do on the other side of the lake. Two demon-possessed men ended up getting free! That means that whatever the wind and the waves were trying to stir up because the enemy knew what was coming, Jesus could rest knowing He was going to end up on the other side! What trust and confidence Jesus had in His Father!

"Then Jesus answered and said to them, '"Most assuredly, I say to you, the Son can do nothing of Himself, but what He sees the Father do; for whatever He does, the Son also does in like manner.'" John 5:19

This is how we move beyond breakthrough. Let's get past just trying to get across the lake when there's a bad storm! Let's have so much peace and trust within our hearts that we rest in Him when the storm arises. Let everyone else freak out because of what is happening. We will rest in Him.

One day my family went for a long hike in the woods about two hours from where we live. Now, my family is used to hiking in the mountains, as we have done that many, many times. This particular time, we decided to go off the beaten path and hike through an area that was recommended on a website, but the path was not clearly marked. After hiking for a while, we realized that we had gotten lost. Thankfully, my phone still worked and was still showing a general GPS location. From the way I understood the GPS, we would have to go through the dense forest to get back to the original location.

I told my family to follow me, because I believed that the GPS was giving an accurate reading, although it was a fairly treacherous way to hike. My son was having a very difficult time with it all and was very scared. It did "feel" like we were lost, but I continued to trust the GPS. We hiked for quite a while, pushing away branches, climbing higher and higher until we all stopped and took a break, exhausted. I looked at my phone again, and everything pointed to the fact we would soon intersect with the original path to get us back to where we had parked. We were worn out, scared and my family was slowly losing the confidence they had placed in me. We got up from where we took our break when all of a sudden, we saw a family come out of nowhere (we never heard them), and they were walking about 20 feet in front of us. They were on the trail that we needed to intersect with to get us out of there! We did it! The GPS did not fail us. Dad did not fail his family. We made it! To this day, my son says that's the most scared he has ever been.

On the drive back to our house (with everyone sleeping in the car) I began to replay the whole event in my mind. I can truly say that I was never scared or worried that we wouldn't make it out, because the GPS kept showing that I was going in the right direction. It didn't make a lot of sense on the map on my phone, but it was tracking my steps, and I kept walking towards what seemed like the original trail.

As we follow God, it's not going to always look good or feel right in the natural. And this is where many people stop and say, "It's too hard. I can't go any further. I'm lost. God, where are you?" If you are going to move beyond breakthrough, you are going to have to learn to trust God with every area of your life. That means your body, your finances, your family, your job and everything else. Beloved, if you are a Christian, you're not lost, even though you may feel like it. Like the hike that I was on, you just need God to lead you back to the path you're supposed to be on. Again, it doesn't mean you're lost into utter darkness (as those who are not born again); it just means that you have strayed from trusting your First Love. You're going to make it. You're going to be alright. Father God can get you through anything!

"When you pass through the waters, I will be with you; And through the rivers, they shall not overflow you. When you walk through the fire, you shall not be burned, nor shall the flame scorch you." Isaiah 43:2

HOW TO DRIVE THE ENEMY CRAZY

Beyond breakthrough is living on the offensive. Beyond breakthrough is to continually take new ground in your life for the Kingdom of Heaven, while at the same time, never giving up any ground to the enemy. We have tried to resist the enemy in our own strength and ability long enough. The enemy has tried to drive us crazy long enough and it's time to take our stand against him, move beyond breakthrough and make him feel crazy frustrated with us to the point where he goes and finds someone else to mess with. We are done with him, and we are going to start keeping the devil on the run from this point forward. This is living beyond breakthrough—it's living daily on the offensive and not putting up with the enemy any longer.

You see, the enemy is afraid of you. He's afraid that at any moment, you are going to "connect all the dots" as you see yourself in the Word of God and what God has promised you and how your future is in Father's hands and not the enemy's. The enemy is afraid that you are going to move beyond breakthrough and start daily living loved, full of joy, full of peace and full of God's presence.

You're going to be prepared now. The enemy is aware of these changes that are about to happen in you, and he's going to try to keep you in a small place and tempt you to think and feel that it's too difficult to move forward in God. But the enemy can't stop you.

"You are of God, little children, and have overcome them, because He who is in you is greater than he who is in the world." 1 John 4:4

From now on, you're not going to allow anything to hold you back from fully pursuing the heart of God!

Now, because the enemy has gone after us for basically our entire lives, we are going to start pursuing him and driving him out of every area of our lives. We are not going to give him any area of our finances, our emotions, our bodies, our minds or our hearts. We are going to make his life miserable; we are going to keep him on the run. We are going to live on the offensive, and every single day, we are going to drive the enemy crazy! Here's how we do that:

FALL IN LOVE

We drive the enemy crazy by keeping the first and greatest commandment first place and living out of this verse throughout the day.

"So He answered and said, "'You shall love the LORD your God with all your heart, with all your soul, with all your strength, and with all your mind, and your neighbor as yourself.'" Luke 10:27

The enemy hates it in when our heart, soul, mind and strength are continually consumed with loving God. He hates it when we daily mediate on our love for God and God's love for us. The enemy does not experience love in any way whatsoever, and he is very jealous that you, a "mere human", would give your love to a God you can't even see. I'm telling you, he hates that!

"whom having not seen you love. Though now you do not see Him, yet believing, you rejoice with joy inexpressible and full of glory," 1 Peter 1:8

The enemy is constantly trying to keep us from loving God with our whole hearts. So, we are going to drive him crazy by loving God with everything within us! I don't know about you, but even as I write this, I feel the love that I have for God flooding my heart!

Father, give us a passionate desire to love you more and more each day!

Every single day, we want to fall in love with Jesus more than the day before. We want there to be such a flow of a love for Jesus coming out of us. Jesus is so good to us, so let's give Him our love from the moment we wake up in the morning until we go to bed at night, and even in the watches of the night.

TRUE SPIRITUAL WARFARE

We drive the enemy crazy by living on the offensive in the spirit. Now, although we do engage in spiritual warfare, we are not supposed to war every moment of every day. Jesus already defeated the enemy and won the victory for us, so now He's trying to *win you over* so He can implement the victory through you. We do fight, we do pray through until we get an answer, we do bind and loose (see Matthew 16:18-19) and so on, but we have to know when to war and when to rest. Every Christian should have a warrior spirit against the enemy where we don't put up with anything he tries to throw at us or our family. We want to daily live on the offensive in every area of our life. We want to live with a posture of always being ready to fight in the spirit when we are called upon. In the meantime, we stand strong against the enemy, never letting him get close:

"Finally, my brethren, be strong in the Lord and in the power of His might. Put on the whole armor of God, that you may be able to stand against the wiles of the devil. For we do not wrestle against flesh and blood, but against principalities, against powers, against the rulers of the darkness of this age, against spiritual hosts of wickedness in the heavenly places. Therefore take up the whole armor of God, that you may be able to withstand in the evil day, and having done

all, to stand." Ephesians 6:10:13

When we are not engaging the enemy, we are standing ready. That's what a good soldier does. They are trained to always be ready at a moment's notice. I know a former black ops soldier who has shared with me some of what he went through when he was in training. It is some of the most intense training you could ever imagine. Although he did not use *all* that he was trained for when he was on missions, he was well-prepared should some of the worst case scenarios ever happen to him. For instance, he was never captured by the enemy on any of his missions, but if you were to hear about the training he went through in case he was ever caught, you would have a renewed gratitude for what these amazing men and women go through to defend our country. He was literally trained for any possible scenario.

I am sharing this with you, because we need to be thoroughly trained to fight the enemy even though we may not find ourselves in a fierce battle every day. Here's how we do it: We learn, meditate on and study healing Scriptures *before* we are sick. We learn, meditate on and study all the joy Scriptures *before* we feel ourselves getting discouraged. And it's the same for every other area of our lives. We practice the presence of the Lord every day *before* a crisis comes our way.

The other day, my daughter was home from college and was not feeling well at all. It was actually a very intense situation. She called me into her room and asked me to pray for her. I prayed, bound the spirit of infirmity and quoted Scriptures, all with no real visible change. Then I began to worship, inviting the presence of the Lord in the room, and I did that for about 15-20 minutes when we both felt the peace of God flood the room. His presence came and took over the situation. The peace was so beautiful that my daughter fell asleep while I was singing over her, and it wasn't too long after that she was fine.

The reason I am sharing this story with you is because the presence that I felt in her room was not foreign to me. I feel that same presence all the time when I pray or worship on my own. I didn't doubt that the Lord was going to visit us in those moments, because I had already been cultivating my relationship with Him when no one was looking. This is so important to understand. We keep the enemy spinning in circles and not knowing what to do with us when, every time he even thinks about coming against us, we worship, quote the Word, stand in faith, plead the blood, count it all joy, walk in love, etc. This is how we drive the enemy crazy. This is how we live beyond breakthrough. So, right now, are you *ready* to fight? Have you cultivated your walk with God? Have you been praying in your heavenly language to strengthen your spirit? Have you stored up your healing Scriptures in your spirit for when you or someone you know is sick? There are many Scriptures at the end of this book that I personalized that you could use to meditate on and fight with!

"Fight the good fight of faith..." 1 Timothy 6:12

It's not about things always coming easy for us in this life. What I am trying to teach you is to always be ready. When things are good, be ready. When things are not so good, be ready. When it's time to do spiritual warfare and push back against the enemy, show him you were already prepared in your spirit. Make him sorry he ever even thought about messing with you! Drive him crazy!

WALKING IN LOVE

We drive the enemy crazy by allowing our hearts to be filled to overflowing with love for one another. To love others is not the first and greatest commandment, but it is second! It's number two on God's list! God takes how we love others very, very seriously. He is closely watching how we love, forgive and treat people. In my book, *"Carrying the Presence"*, I go into great detail about how we are to love one another because of an encounter that I had with Jesus in Heaven. He talked to me about how I needed to work on my love and then downloaded to me how to practically walk that out on earth.

The enemy is also watching how we love, react, forgive and treat others. When we chose to love others and not live in offense, bitterness and unforgiveness, that gives the enemy no foothold in us towards others. And this drives him crazy.

"And above all things have fervent love for one another, for

'"love will cover a multitude of sins."' 1 Peter 4:8

The enemy will try and try to get you to not walk in love towards others, because when we don't have love, how are we going to reach those around us? How are we going to minster to our family, church members or strangers when our hearts are not full of love for people?

"Owe no one anything except to love one another, for he who loves another has fulfilled the law." Romans 13:8

The truth is, it all goes back to living daily in the love of God. It's not possible to live and walk in God's love and have a disdain for others. You will love others to the extent that you feel loved and enjoyed by God. Let that sink in for a moment.

Beloved, pass the test of love:

"Love suffers long and is kind; love does not envy; love does not parade itself, is not puffed up; does not behave rudely, does not seek its own, is not provoked, thinks no evil; does not rejoice in iniquity, but rejoices in the truth; bears all things, believes all things, hopes all things, endures all things. Love never fails..." 1 Corinthians 13:4-8

Love comes before all the other fruits of the spirit, because they are all born out of love. For instance, if you try really hard to be more patient, that doesn't mean you are necessarily walking in greater love. However, when you walk in greater love, you will become more patient with others, because patience flows from love and not the other way around.

If you took to heart the portion of this book about healing the heart, it will be much easier for you to love others. We want to love others the way we want to be loved.

The Bible says that others will know we are Christians by our, anointing? Our preaching? Our intelligence? No, by our love (See John 13:35).

Drive the enemy crazy by being quick to love and quick to forgive!

"The Peter came to Him and said, '"Lord, how often shall my brother sin against me, and I forgive him? Up to seven times?"' Jesus said to him, '"I do not say to you, up to seven times, but up to seventy times seven."' Matthew 18:21-22

THE BLOOD OF JESUS

We drive the enemy crazy by reminding him of the precious and powerful blood of Jesus! We need to get into the habit of speaking often of the blood of Jesus, reminding the enemy that it's because of the shed blood of Jesus that he has been utterly defeated. Every day as it comes to your remembrance, thank Jesus for the blood that He shed for you, and this will keep the devil on the run. Even now, lift up your hands, and out loud say, "Jesus, I thank You for Your blood! You hear that devil? The blood of Jesus has defeated you! Jesus, thank You for shedding Your blood for me!"

Jesus' blood is enough to keep you in a place of victory and freedom. The enemy hates the blood of Jesus, so that's why we want to drive him crazy by reminding him of it often.

Here's a few verses to remind yourself and the enemy of the blood of Jesus (it wouldn't hurt to speak these out loud; the enemy hates it!):

"In Him we have redemption through His blood, the forgiveness of sins, according to the riches of His grace" Eph. 1:7

"and by Him to reconcile all things to Himself, by Him, whether things on earth or things in heaven, having made peace through the blood of His cross." Colossians 1:20

"Therefore, brethren, having boldness to enter the Holiest by the blood of Jesus," Hebrews 10:19

"Then He took the cup, and gave thanks, and gave it to them, saying, '"Drink from it, all of you. For this is My blood of the new covenant, which is shed for many for the remission of sins."' Mat.26:27-28

"And they overcame him by the blood of the Lamb and by the word of their testimony, and they did not love their lives to the death." Rev. 12:11

THE POWER OF YOUR TESTIMONY

We drive the enemy crazy by unashamedly sharing the

testimonies of how Jesus has saved us, set us free, healed us and brought us through! I thoroughly wrote about this in Chapter 5, so let me share with you a sweet story I heard once:

The story goes that there was a young minister at the house of an old saint of God. She was up in years, and her Bible was virtually worn out. The young minister opened her tattered Bible and noticed that throughout the Bible, there was the letter "T" next to a particular verse. And then next to many of the letter "T"s was also written the letter "P". The inquisitive minister asked the beloved intercessor what the letters meant. She said, "Oh son, the letter 'T' stands for the word 'TRIED'. It means I TRIED this verse over many years of living for God. I TRIED it over and over again." The minister then said, "And next to most of the letter 'T's is the letter 'P'. What does this mean?" The precious woman said with great authority, "'T' means I TRIED it and 'P' means that God PROVED it!"

I'm sure that old saint had dozens, if not hundreds, of testimonies of what God had brought her through. When was last time you shared one of your testimonies with someone? Ask the Lord to give you an opportunity to share with someone the goodness of God in your life. Every time you share your testimony, it drives the enemy crazy, because you are reminding him of what God can do for His children. Always be bold to share with others how God has changed your life!

SHARING JESUS

Do you want to drive the enemy crazy? I know you do. This is a very important one. We drive the enemy crazy by being a witness and sharing the Good News of Jesus with the world around us. This is premise of my book, *"Carrying The Presence"* where I share the revelation on what it really means to carry the presence of God with us wherever we go. This is beyond just sharing your testimony; it's telling a precious lost and dark soul that Jesus loves them and has a plan for their life. It's such a privilege to be used by God to turn someone from the kingdom of darkness to the kingdom of light. All that we are able to bring to Heaven with us are those people who the Holy Spirit directed us to share Jesus with.

You can see how this would drive the enemy crazy. What once belonged to the enemy now belongs to Jesus, and you were a part of that. As I mentioned previously in this book, one of the enemy's biggest goals is to keep us so self-focused through all that we go through in life that we do not have anything left for the world around us. But I know you would agree that's all about to change after what you learned through this book.

My friends, share the love of Jesus to the world around you on a regular basis. Make the devil nervous and afraid of the fact that you just walked into work, a restaurant, a gas station, or the mall, and that at any moment, you could tell a complete stranger that Jesus loves them! Just open up your mouth, and the Holy Spirit will take care of the rest—it's that simple. This drives the enemy so crazy!

In fact, why don't you get a head start right now on sharing Jesus with someone. Take just a moment and think about the people in your life that you see on a regular basis. It could be someone that works at the coffee shop or at the place you work...anywhere. Try to think of ten different people that you know you would like to share Jesus with. Now, I have given you a few lines for you to write down their name (if you don't know their name, just write how you know them) to help you to remember to pray for them. Then be ready and prepared for the open door to share Jesus with them!

YOUR TOP TEN LIST

_____

_____

_____

_____

_____

_____

_____

_____

_____

_____

_____

_____

_____

_____

_____

_____

_____

_____

_____

_____

_____

_____

_____

_____

_____

_____

_____

_____

_____

_____

_____

_____

_____

_____

As I said earlier, you are the answer to the Lord's prayer.

YOUR HEAVENLY LANGUAGE

Another way that we drive the enemy crazy is by praying in

the Spirit, our heavenly language, all throughout the day.

"But you, beloved, building yourselves up on your most holy faith, praying in the Holy Spirit" Jude 20

My dear friend, Kevin Zadai likes to share how Jesus visited him once and said that praying in the Spirit is the most supernatural thing we can do as Christians. The spiritual benefits of praying in tongues is a whole other book in itself. I believe that the enemy has no idea what's truly taking place when we are praying in our heavenly language, and he hates that and tries to fight to keep us from doing it.

"pray without ceasing" 1 Thessalonians 5:17

Praying in our heavenly language is how we are able to pray without ceasing. I can testify that my life has been completely changed by praying in the Spirit as much as possible throughout the day. I challenge you to do the same, and watch what begins to happen for you. And yes, it drives the enemy crazy and shifts your life to the point that you move beyond breakthrough!

If you do not yet have this beautiful gift of praying in your Heavenly language, just know that this gift is available for all those who believe in Jesus. When you are able to find a time to get alone and pray, ask the Lord to fill you will the Holy Spirit with the evidence of speaking in tongues. It will come from your spirit and not your mind. In other words, it will just flow out of you. The important thing is that you simply open up your mouth and begin to speak what is coming up from within. When we ask, we receive. We just have to ask in faith like a little child!

"He who speaks in a tongue edifies himself…" 1 Corinthians 14:4

WORSHIP AT ALL TIMES

Being a worshipper of Jesus drives the enemy crazy. The enemy can't be around worship and praise, not at all. Don't you just love the thought that? If you stay in worship, the enemy doesn't stick around! You see, the enemy is the one that wants all the attention on himself and doesn't want you to fix your gaze on Jesus in the good times or the bad. When we give thanks, praise and worship to Jesus on a regular basis, not only will the enemy flee from you, but you will experience God's presence in greater dimensions! This is another way that we move beyond breakthrough and into ongoing encounters in His presence.

"I will bless the LORD at all times; His praise shall continually be in my mouth." Psalm 34:1

King David knew how to worship God. He actually wrote that verse while going through his own trial. When we worship God while in the midst of a trial, we are drawing attention away from what we are going through and focusing our hearts on Jesus. This does not mean that the trial is no longer there, but what you are doing is setting your heart and affections on Jesus rather than the trial.

Whenever I find myself up against a trial, I know that I know that if I will just *choose* to bless the Lord—if I *choose* to worship—God will visit me. You see when our hearts are overwhelmed and grieved, when we feel discouraged or feel like giving up, when we feel defeated or in fear, the truth is, it's not easy to worship. But WE MUST press through. Every single time, without fail, that I have chosen to spend time worshipping Jesus while in the midst of a crisis, He has always come and stilled my heart and given me peace.

When we worship, Jesus visits us, and the enemy leaves. Again, the enemy can't be around our worship of the Lord, so why not do it more often?

Worship brings His presence. Worship draws us ever closer to His heart. Worship settles an unsettled heart. When we choose to worship while in the midst of a trial, this is very precious to the Lord. He knows you're hurting and discouraged, and yet you choose to worship Him, because He is good through it all. He loves it. He loves you. You see, it's easy to worship, praise and adore what delights us. The more we live in communion with Jesus, the easier it will be to worship Him "at all times".

DON'T LOSE YOUR JOY!

We drive the enemy crazy by keeping a joyful and glad heart through all circumstances. I know that's not always easy, but it would not be in the Word if it was not possible.

"My brethren, count it all joy when you fall into various trials" James 1:2

An authentic joyful and glad heart comes from a deep, inner assurance that no matter what the circumstances around me may be saying, no matter how the enemy is trying to take me out, Father God still has me in the palm of His hand, and He will see me through.

Fullness of joy and gladness of heart come from spending time with Jesus. It seems that I am always taken by surprise when I spend time with someone that seems so joyful (that authentic contagious type of joy), and then I hear their life story, and it's a rough one. Somewhere along the way, they found the secret of a joyful and glad heart. Their pain and heartache were replaced with joy and gladness, and it seems that that type of Christian can never be shaken. That person has moved beyond breakthrough and into deep joy and gladness of heart.

"You have put gladness in my heart, more than in the season that their grain and wine increased." Psalm 4:7

Did you know that Jesus was anointed with gladness more than anyone else?

"You have loved righteousness and hated lawlessness; Therefore God, Your God, has anointed You with the oil of gladness more than Your companions." Hebrews 1:9

Jesus is so full of joy and gladness. Today, laugh at the enemy. Laugh until you know that you know he heard you, and drive him crazy!

GIVERS VS. TAKERS

Another way that we drive the enemy crazy is when we live a lifestyle of giving and not taking. I'm not just talking about giving money, even though that's a big part of it, because money has such a hold on people. If you are gifted as a mechanic, when was the last time you worked on someone's car expecting nothing in return? The enemy hates that. If you are a good handyman, when was the last time you helped someone in your church who doesn't have a lot of money, and you simply and joyfully helped them because you know they can't pay you back? The enemy hates those who are unselfish.

We all need to learn to be a greater blessing to others, especially to those who can't do anything for you in return.

"And remember the words of the Lord Jesus, that He said, 'It is more blessed to give than to receive.'" Acts 20:35

When you are a giver of your finances, time, resources and talent, expecting nothing in return, you are acknowledging that Jesus is your source, and nothing you have owns you or has an unhealthy grip on you. You are literally storing up treasures in Heaven by becoming a joyful giver. If you learn to be a giver, Father God will see to it that you are blessed in this life and in the life to come. No matter how small it is, when we give from a pure heart, Heaven takes notice and will reward you. Giving drives the enemy crazy.

KEEP YOUR SWORD SHARP

We drive the enemy crazy by keeping our Sword—the very Word of God—sharp and by using it on a regular basis.

"For the word of God is living and powerful, and sharper than any two-edged sword, piercing even to the division of soul and spirit, and of joints and marrow, and is a discerner of the thoughts and intents of the heart." Hebrews 4:12

Whatever problem or situation you are facing, there is a promise in Scripture that you can hold on to and fight the enemy with. To use a particular Scripture is to take out your sword and use it cut down the enemy.

What are you facing right now? Get yourself a couple of Scriptures to back you up and say, "Hey devil, 1 Peter 2:24 says that by the stripes of Jesus I was healed! So, you spirit of infirmity, I'm going to drive you crazy with this verse, and I'm going to keep reminding you that Jesus is my Healer until I'm healed!" Or you may say, "You know what devil? You have attacked my finances long enough, the Bible says in Philippians 4:19, that my Father supplies every one of my needs, so enough is enough. I am going to drive you crazy with the promises of God for my finances!"

Do you see how knowing, receiving and quoting the Word is

like taking out a sword against the enemy? Any lie the enemy is whispering to you, any desperate situation that you are finding yourself in, anything you need is found in the Word of God. Meditate on the Word daily so you are always ready to fight.

"But his delight is in the law of the LORD, and in His law he meditates day and night." Psalm 1:2

In the next chapter, I listed a number of declarations that you can use to sharpen you Sword.

KEEP YOUR PEACE

We drive the enemy crazy by living in peace and not stress, worry or anxiety. These days that we live in can be very stressful. And if we are not careful, we will find ourselves yielding to the stress that we face each day. We have to learn to keep our peace. The enemy hates peace. He wants chaos, confusion and worry to be part of your life so that you are not able to hear God's voice and discern the season you are in with God. The God-kind of peace comes from an inner knowing that because you know Father God, He's going to work everything out for your good.

"Be anxious for nothing, but in everything by prayer and supplication, with thanksgiving, let your requests be made known to God; and the peace of God, which surpasses all understanding, will guard your hearts and minds through Christ Jesus." Philippians 4:6-7

My Pastor from my time at the Brownsville Revival, John Kilpatrick, preached one of the greatest sermons that I have ever heard. It was entitled, "Everything is Father Filtered." In other words, nothing takes Father God by surprise that happens in our lives. Somehow, it's all going to work together for good (see Romans 8:28).

Keep your peace, and don't be easily shaken.

"Peace I leave with you, My peace I give to you; not as the world gives do I give to you. Let not your heart be troubled, neither let it be afraid." John 14:27

The enemy hates a Christian that walks in peace! So, don't worry about tomorrow, and walk in the peace of Jesus today.

"Therefore do not worry, saying, 'What shall we eat?' or 'What shall we drink?' or 'What shall we wear?' For after all these things the Gentiles seek. For your heavenly Father knows that you need all these things. But seek first the kingdom of God and His righteousness, and all these things shall be added to you. Therefore do not worry about tomorrow, for tomorrow will worry about its own things. Sufficient for the day is its own trouble." Matthew 6:31-34

NEVER, EVER GIVE UP

We drive the enemy crazy by never, ever, giving up and throwing in the towel. The truth is, if you give up, the enemy wins. I'm not saying you won't go to Heaven, but in this life on earth, the enemy wins when we give up. Evangelist Mario Murillo said once, "Life is not hard, it's impossible!" And that's true if we don't keep Jesus at the forefront of every part of our lives.

We have to make a choice every day that we are going to keep going after the heart of God! We have to keep our hearts burning with passion for Jesus. I know you have been tired, maybe beat up, let down, misunderstood, wounded, sick, frustrated, discouraged, stressed out or overwhelmed, but I am reminding you today, DO NOT give up.

"And let us not grow weary while doing good, for in due season we shall reap if we do not lose heart." Galatians 6:9

If you stay faithful, you will reap a harvest of what you have been praying, thanking, declaring, interceding and worshipping God for. Remember all the Rocky Balboa movies? How many times did he get knocked down in all the movies to just get back up and fight again? There is more fight in you than you realize, because Jesus lives inside you.

"But without faith it is impossible to please Him, for he who comes to God must believe that He is, and that He is a rewarder of those who diligently seek Him." Hebrews 11:6

John Paul Jones, a Revolutionary War Naval Commander in the late 1700's, was in an intense battle with another ship, and when everything around him seemed like an unfavorable outcome, John Paul Jones said, "I have not yet begun to fight!"

I love that statement. No matter what your situation looks like right now, you stare the enemy down and say, "Devil, as a Christian and beloved child of God, I have not yet begun to fight!" This will drive the enemy crazy, because he thought he had you!

ORDINARY MOMENTS

God is not just found in church services, prayer meetings, worship gatherings, Bible schools or Bible studies. God is found in the ordinary moments of life—the ordinary moments of mowing the lawn, changing diapers, going out to eat, pumping gas, sitting at the DMV, flying on a plane, driving to work, and the thousands upon thousands of other ordinary moments in our lives. If we learn one of the biggest secrets of the Christian life, that we can encounter God in even the most ordinary and mundane moments of life, we have won half the battle. The enemy does not want you to ever figure out that we can encounter God anytime, anywhere. Father God loves to reveal Himself to us in the "ordinariness" of life. Why? Because the ordinary moments of life are where we live most of the time.

The reality is that between the "mountain top experiences" of life are large valleys of ordinary moments. But friend, we can experience God just as beautifully in the valley as on the mountaintop!

I know life can be so crazy at times. We have bills to pay, kids to raise, places to go, people to see, ministry to do, relationships to build, work to be done around the house, a job to go, emails to answer, social media, living healthy, etc.—and that's just on a Monday! Again, these are some of life's "ordinary moments".

I have come to a place in my life where, if I am going to do all these ordinary things, then I would rather do them with Jesus, living in His presence, enjoying His love and walking in joy, rather than getting upset, overwhelmed, burned out, stressed out, discouraged, anxious, fearful and the like. And I am convinced that He has made a way for us to come to that sacred place where we can enjoy Him 24/7.

Have you ever seen the movie, "Mr. Magorium's Wonder Emporium"? It's a cute movie with many undertones of life lessons. It's definitely worth watching. Without giving away too much, there is scene in the movie where the main character is about to leave this world to head for another. In the meantime, he is trying to teach a young lady how important it is to enjoy the little things of life. While in a clock shop, they both set every clock to go off at the same time so all the chimes could be heard simultaneously. Here's the dialogue from the movie of the two of them after Mr. Magorium sets the last clock:

Mr. Magorium: "That's the last of 'em, 37 seconds."

Mahoney (young lady): "Great. Well done. Now we wait."

Mr. Magorium: "No. We breathe. We pulse. We regenerate. Our hearts beat. Our minds create. Our souls ingest. 37 seconds, well used, is a lifetime."

That whole interaction really touches me. Friends, because of the relationship we have with Jesus, even the most mundane and ordinary moments of life can turn into extraordinary encounters in the presence of the Lord.

So, drive the enemy really, really crazy by learning to enjoy the Lord every day and in the ordinary moments of life. Worship while you're doing the dishes. Pray in your heavenly language while driving to work. Share Jesus with someone while getting groceries, pray for someone while mowing the lawn, and let the Lord love on you while you are walking the dog. This is one of the greatest ways to move beyond breakthrough!

GET OVER YOURSELF

Every day, give yourself afresh to the Lord. Present yourself before Him and say, "Here I am Lord. I love you, I am all Yours, and I'm ready to serve and obey you today." You know, Jesus longs to hear that more often from those who love Him. Let's not just say that we love God; let's demonstrate our love for Him by denying ourselves, our plans, our desires and yield to whatever He has for us to do day by day.

"I beseech you therefore, brethren, by the mercies of God,

that you present your bodies a living sacrifice, holy, acceptable to God, which is your reasonable service. And do not be conformed to this world, but be transformed by the renewing of your mind, that you may prove what is that good and acceptable and perfect will of God." Romans 12:1-2

We drive the enemy crazy when we choose to deny ourselves and love and serve God above everything else in life. We demonstrate our heart and commitment to God as His faithful disciples when we live this way.

"Then He said to them all, '"If anyone desires to come after Me, let him deny himself, and take up his cross daily, and follow Me."' Luke 9:23

Here's something that you don't hear preached much in the 21st century; the crucified life. I have found that in the grace and love of God, living the crucified life is a joy and not a drain. We must get to the place where we simply love the Lord so much that we wouldn't want to do or say anything that doesn't please His heart.

"I have been crucified with Christ; it is no longer I who live, but Christ lives in me; and the life which I now live in the flesh I live by faith in the Son of God, who loved me and gave Himself for me." Galatians 2:20

When you love someone, I mean really love someone, you live a life of self-denial and self-sacrifice towards that person. The enemy hates it when we live this way, because we are choosing to put God and others above ourselves. Understand that there is a grace and strength to live this way (of self-denial) that flows from a heart of unending love for Jesus. Sometimes we have to just look in the mirror and say, "You know what, it's time to get over myself. It's not all about me." This is another way we begin to live beyond breakthrough!

STAY ENCOURAGED

The first book I ever wrote was, "How to Encourage Yourself in the Lord" (you can find this book on Amazon). I wrote that book to teach people to do what David did when everything around him was falling apart in 1 Samuel 30. David knew how to encourage Himself in the Lord when he was going through it. He had to do this many times in his life as the enemy was constantly after him. We drive the enemy crazy when in the midst of all that we are going through, we throw up our hands and worship the Lord and stand on the promises of God.

When we choose to encourage ourselves in the Lord, there is an exchange that takes place as I give the Lord all that I am going through, and in the exchange, He gives me His peace, love, joy and the answers that I need in the moment. The enemy can't stand Christians that choose to encourage themselves in the Lord rather than letting the enemy walk all over them and make them feel defeated.

Next time you are going through a rough patch, choose to encourage yourself in the Lord, and watch how your spirit is lifted up above the circumstances!

PURE IN HEART

This one is at the top of the list of what drives the enemy crazy!

"Blessed are the pure in heart, for they shall see God."
Matthew 5:8

Beloved, the pure—not the perfect—but the pure in heart see and encounter God. This is very, very important to the Lord. A pure heart is a heart that keeps short accounts with the Lord. In other words, you are quick to say, "Forgive me Jesus". A pure heart has no ulterior motives, unforgiveness, lust, bitterness, secret sin or any other destructive behavior hidden within it.

Beloved, there is nothing like living with a pure heart. There is nothing like living clean before God. We are righteous before God (see 2 Corinthians 5:21) because we are children of God, but if we want to *see* God, our hearts must remain pure. Again, this is not about being perfect, but pure. It's a heart with no duplicity. This is very precious to the Lord. The enemy hates purity, because with purity comes favor from the Lord.

"For the LORD God is a sun and shield; The LORD will give grace and glory; No good thing will He withhold from those who

walk uprightly." Psalm 84:11

LIVE LOVED

And finally, we drive the enemy crazy by receiving and living in the Father's love every day. My friend, He loves you so much. Do you believe that? Have you received that truth? Right now is the perfect time to draw closer to Jesus than you have ever been and learn to live daily in His love.

"There is no fear in love; but perfect love casts out fear, because fear involves torment. But he who fears has not been made perfect in love." 1 John 4:18

We all must have a divine revelation of Father's love in this hour. This perfect love that we read about only comes from the Father, for He *is* perfect love. And when we live in the revelation that each one of us is deeply loved, cherished and adored by God, then we can live this life in great confidence within our hearts, no matter what is going on around us.

Did you know that right now, you are literally surrounded by His love? Here's what Paul the Apostle said:

"that He would grant you, according to the riches of His glory, to be strengthened with might through His Spirit in the inner man, that Christ may dwell in your hearts through faith; that you, being rooted and grounded in love, may be able to comprehend with all the saints what is the width and length and depth and height— to know the love of Christ which passes knowledge; that you may be filled with all the

fullness of God. Now to Him who is able to do exceedingly abundantly above all that we ask or think, according to the power that works in us" Ephesians 3:16-20

Did you catch that? Paul spoke of the width, length, depth and height of God's love. That means that you are surrounded by His love right now! You may say, "Ryan, I believe what you are saying, and I believe the Word of God, but for some reason, I can't seem to encounter His love for myself." I can relate, because I have been there, like I wrote previously.

"keep yourselves in the love of God..." Jude 21

To keep yourself in His love is to learn to be a good receiver of His love and to choose to never let anything rob you of living loved. It is from this position of love that we are able to face ANYTHING the enemy tries to take us out with. To be loved, to feel loved and to live loved by Father God is one of the greatest privileges that we possess as children of God.

What I want you to know about Father's love is that the very essence of how He thinks is love. The essence of how He feels is love. He thinks with burning love. He feels with burning love. Even His judgments and disciplines are all about removing everything that hinders love. There is no contradiction between His judgment, His discipline and His love.

"As the Father loved Me, I also have loved you; abide in My

love." John 15:9

We have to learn to continually take refuge in Father's love. Run to Him like a little child. He loves that!

Beloved, we will never exhaust the vast ocean of Father's love, but we will forever experience new aspects of it. Like John the Beloved, we lean back into Jesus (see John 21:20) when we have questions, when we need to feel loved, when we are weary, dry and hurting, or when we just need to be embraced by His love.

We must get Father's perspective of who we are, what we have gone through, what we are going through and where we are headed. When we live loved, it gives us the confidence that each one of us can see ourselves as "God's favorite!"

Rest in His love. Live in His love. Let Him embrace you and speak loving words to your heart. He is the perfect Father, full of joy and happiness over you, dancing over you (see Zephaniah 3:17), cheering you on, encouraging your heart. Forever be a student of the heart of God!

To live loved is to move beyond breakthrough!

8

DECLARATIONS

"God never made a promise that was too good to be true."
D.L. Moody

I compiled these personalized verses for you to use as worship to God, as an encouragement to your heart and as a weapon against the enemy. Read them all often, or grab ahold of one or two and meditate on them continually until they become part of you. You are loved!

I thank You that You have made ALL things new in my life! (2 Cor. 5:17)

I only do those things that please my Father today! (John 8:29)

I am complete in Him Who is the Head of all principality and power. (Colossians 2:10)

I am surrounded by a shield of favor (Psalm 5:12)

I have forsaken all and taken up my cross and am following You. (Luke 14:26-33)

I am alive with Christ. (Ephesians 2:5)

My identity is rooted in being loved and being a lover of God! (John 14:21)

I am free from the law of sin and death. (Romans 8:2)

I thank You that as I seek You with all my heart, I will find You! (Jer. 29:11-13)

I ask and it shall be given unto me, I seek and I shall find, I knock and it shall be opened to me. (Matthew 7:7,8)

I am far from oppression, and fear does not come near me. (Isaiah 54:14)

I abhor what is evil today, and I cling to that which is good. (Romans 12:9)

I walk in the wisdom of God today. (James 1:5)

You, O Lord, are a shield for me, my glory and the One who lifts up my head. (Ps. 3:3)

I declare today that I love God with ALL my heart, mind, soul and strength. (Luke 10:27)

I walk in the Spirit today, and I do not fulfill the lusts and desires of the flesh. (Gal. 5:16)

You have come that I would have life more abundantly. (John 10:10)

I am born of God, and the evil one does not touch me. (I John 5:18)

I will not worry today or be anxious. (Phil. 4:6)

I declare that the love of God has been poured out in my heart by the Holy Spirit who was given to me. (Romans 5:5)

I am holy and without blame before Him in love. (I Peter 1:16; Ephesians 1:4)

I trust in the Lord today with ALL MY HEART, and I do not lean on my own understanding. IN ALL MY WAYS, I will acknowledge Him, and He will direct my paths. (Proverbs 3:5,6)

I will pray without ceasing. (1 Thess. 5:17)

I will praise without ceasing! (Psalm 34:1)

I have the mind of Christ. (Philippians 2:5; I Corinthians 2:16).

I receive the fullness of God's love today! (Eph. 3:17-19)

You work ALL THINGS together for good, because I love You, and I am called according to Your purposes. (Romans 8:28)

I have the peace of God that passes all understanding. (Philippians 4:7)

You are keeping me in perfect peace, because my mind is stayed on You. (Is. 26:3)

I have the Greater One living in me; greater is He Who is in me than he who is in the world. (I John 4:4)

I declare today that NOTHING is too hard or impossible for God. (Luke 1:37)

I walk in the strength of the joy of the Lord today. (Nem. 8:10)

I declare today that His banner over me is LOVE, LOVE, LOVE! (Song of Songs 2:4)

I call unto the Lord, and He shall answer me and show me great and mighty things! (Jer. 33:3)

I walk in the prophetic today. (1 Cor. 14:1)

I hear the voice of God today. (John 10:4-5)

I walk in Divine appointments. (Ps. 37:23)

I have received the gift of righteousness and reign as a king in life through Jesus Christ. (Romans 5:17)

The Blessing of God has overtaken me! (Deut. 28:2)

As I wait on the Lord today, my strength is renewed, and I shall mount up with wings like eagles. I shall run and not grow weary, and I shall walk and not faint. (Is. 40:31)

This is the day that the Lord has made, and I will rejoice and be glad in it! (Ps. 118:24)

I have received the spirit of wisdom and revelation in the knowledge of Jesus, the eyes of my understanding being enlightened. (Ephesians 1:17,18)

I am CONFIDENT of this very thing, that He who has begun a good work in me will complete it until the day of Jesus Christ. (Phil.1:6)

I have the tongue of the learned that I should know how to speak a word in season. (Is. 50:4)

I walk in the Isaiah 61 mandate today. (Is. 61)

I have received the power of the Holy Spirit to lay hands on the sick and see them recover, to cast out demons, and to speak with new tongues. I have power over all the power of the enemy, and nothing shall by any means harm me. (Mark 16:17,18; Luke 10:17,19)

I am free from all condemnation, because I am in Christ Jesus. (Romans 8:1)

I thank You that everything that I set my hand to do is blessed! (Deut. 28:12)

I have put off the old man and have put on the new man, which is renewed in knowledge after the image of Him Who created me. (Colossians 3:9,10)

I put on the whole armor of God today. (Eph. 6:11-17)

I declare that NO weapon formed against me or my family today will prosper, and every tongue that rises up against us in judgment shall be condemned. (Is. 54:17)

I present my body today as a living sacrifice, holy, acceptable to God which is my reasonable service. (Romans 12:1)

I will not be conformed to this world, but I will be transformed by the renewing of my mind. (Romans 12:2)

I have given, and it is given to me; good measure, pressed down, shaken together, and running over, men give into my bosom. (Luke 6:38)

I have NO LACK, because God supplies all my needs according to His riches in glory by Christ Jesus. (Philippians 4:19)

I can quench all the fiery darts of the wicked one with my shield of faith. (Ephesians 6:16)

I can do all things through Christ Jesus who gives me strength. (Philippians 4:13)

I shall do even greater works than Christ Jesus. (John 14:12)

I show forth the praises of God who has called me out of darkness into His marvelous light. (I Peter 2:9)

I will bless the Lord at ALL times; His praise shall continually be in my mouth. (Psalm 34:1)

I am God's child—for I am born again of the incorruptible seed of the Word of God, which lives and abides forever. (I Peter 1:23)

I am a person after God's own heart! (Acts 13:22)

I am God's workmanship, created in Christ unto good works. (Ephesians 2:10)

I am a new creature in Christ. (II Corinthians 5:17)

I am a spirit being—alive to God. (I Thessalonians 5:23; Romans 6:11)

I am a believer, and the light of the Gospel shines in my mind. (II Corinthians 4:4)

I declare that my family is debt free! (Phil. 4:19)

I am a doer of the Word and blessed in my actions. (James 1:22,25)

I am a joint-heir with Christ. (Romans 8:17)

I am more than a conqueror through Him who loves me. (Romans 8:37)

I am an overcomer by the blood of the Lamb and the word of my testimony. (Revelation 12:11)

I am a partaker of His divine nature. (II Peter 1:3,4)

I am an ambassador for Christ. (II Corinthians 5:20)

I am the righteousness of God in Jesus Christ. (2 Cor. 5:21)

I am part of a chosen generation, a royal priesthood, a holy nation, a purchased people. (I Peter 2:9)

I am the temple of the Holy Spirit; I am not my own. (I Corinthians 6:19)

I am the head and not the tail; I am above only and not beneath. (Deuteronomy 28:13)

I am the light of the world. (Matthew 5:14)

I am the salt of the earth. (Matthew 5:13)

I am His elect, full of mercy, kindness, humility, and longsuffering. (Romans 8:33; Colossians 3:12)

I owe a debt of love to everyone today. (Rom. 13:8)

I am forgiven of ALL my sins and washed in the blood. (Ephesians 1:7 1John 1:9)

God has REMOVED my sins as far as the east is from the west. (Ps.103:12)

I am delivered from the power of darkness and translated into God's kingdom. (Colossians 1:13)

I am redeemed from the curse of sin, sickness, and poverty. (Galatians 3:13; Deuteronomy 28:15-68)

I am firmly rooted, built up, established in my faith, and overflowing with gratitude. (Colossians 2:7)

I am called of God to be the voice of His praise. (II Timothy 1:9; Psalm 66:8)

I am healed by the stripes of Jesus and I walk in divine health. (I Peter 2:24; Isaiah 53:5)

I am raised up with Christ and seated in heavenly places. (Colossians 2:12; Ephesians 2:6)

I am GREATLY loved by God. (Colossians 3:12; Romans 1:7; I Thessalonians 1:4; Ephesians 2:4)

I am strengthened with all might according to His glorious power. (Colossians 1:11)

I am submitted to God, and the devil flees from me because I resist him in the name of Jesus. (James 4:7)

I am strong in the Lord and in the power of His might. (Eph. 6:10)

I press on toward the goal to win the prize to which God in Christ Jesus is calling us upward. (Philippians 3:14)

For God has not given me a spirit of fear, but of power, love, and a sound mind. (II Timothy 1:7)

It is not I who live, but Christ lives in me (Galatians 2:20).

I declare that NOTHING shall separate me from the love of God! (Romans 8:38,39)

I keep myself in the LOVE OF GOD today! (Jude 21)

ABOUT THE AUTHOR

Revive International was founded by Ryan Bruss to take the Gospel of Jesus Christ to the nations of the world. Ryan has had the privilege of traveling to many countries, seeing people saved, healed, and delivered! With a passion for revival and the Father heart of God, he has seen the power of God in salvations, prophecy, and miracles - from house churches to open air meetings. Besides traveling to minister, Ryan, along with an amazing group of passionate believers, pastors a church in North Carolina called Antioch Community Church. Ryan and his beautiful wife Megan have been married for over 21 years and have two wonderful kids, Elianna and Andrew.

If you would like Ryan to come and minister, please contact us at: reviveus247@gmail.com or you can visit our websites at: www.reviveus.org or www.antiochcommunitychurch.org

KILLING LAZARUS

Printed in Great Britain
by Amazon